A Guide for the Church Usher

A Guide for the Church Usher

Thomas L. Clark

BROADMAN
&HOLMAN
PUBLISHERS

Library of Congress Cataloging in Publication Data

Clark, Thomas L., 1938-
   A guide for the church usher.

   1. Church ushers—Handbooks, manuals, etc.
I. Title.
BV705.C57   1984   254   83-26211
ISBN 0-8054-3517-4

© Copyright 1984 • Broadman Press
All rights reserved
4235-17
ISBN: 0-8054-3517-4
Dewey Decimal Classification: 254
Subject Heading: USHERS
Library of Congress Catalog Number: 83-26211
Printed in the United States of America

                12 06 05 04

Contents

Dedicated
to those faithful servants, the church ushers,
who honor their Lord and serve his church
and especially
to my dad, H. S. Clark, and father-in-law, R. J. Shelton,
who both understand what it means to be a church usher.

Introduction

Some of my earliest recollections of attending church focus on the big people who talked with my parents, gave them pieces of paper, walked with them into the sanctuary, and picked at me. Soon I came to know these people as my friends and looked forward to seeing them each week at church. As a child, I learned that these happy people were church ushers.

During my youth years, I was allowed to serve as an usher as a part of special emphasis weeks in my church. I didn't fully understand the role or function of being an usher, but I had fun and have many wonderful memories of those special times.

As a college and seminary student, I was a member of churches that had fine ushers. I noticed the joy in the ushers' lives and felt their warmth and concern. They knew my name and always had a kind word to say.

After I was ordained into the gospel ministry and went to my first church, ushers became closely tied to my work. I continued to learn their roles and functions. I counted on them for help. They responded wonderfully to my requests and added much to my life.

I have been served by ushers in big and small churches, with a variety of ethnic backgrounds—male and female, young and old—all are a part of my total experience.

These pages are written to you, a church usher, as though we were talking face-to-face. The ideas in this book have been shared with me through the years by ushers like you. Some of the ideas will be familiar; a few will be new; but all will need to be translated into the way you do things in your church.

Someday our paths may cross. I may attend your church and be ushered by you. I'll want to meet you personally and thank you for being a part of a world-wide fellowship.

Happy ushering.

THOMAS L. CLARK
Nashville, Tennessee

1
A Place to Serve

The time is 11:10 AM. The day is Sunday. You are standing at the front door of your church. You spot a car pulling into the parking lot. You notice the out-of-state license tag. Shortly, a young couple with a baby in the mother's arms get out of the car and make their way to the front door of the church.

This is not an unusual scene for any church on any given Sunday morning. How you respond to this scene will depend on who you are. If you are late to church and just checking on the weather outside, you will notice the couple and go on to the service. However, if you are an usher, your action will be quite different.

Long before the scene described above happens, many events have placed you at the front door of your church. You are an usher and

- You have been selected by your church to serve
- You have considered the responsibilities of being an usher
- You have been trained for your place of service
- You are in your place to serve.

Selected by Your Church

In most churches, ushers are selected by a nominating committee and elected by the church members. The committee gives careful thought to their
selections. As time allows, the committee considers
the role and functions of the usher before making
their selections. Some churches have a job description
written for the church usher, and this becomes a
guide for the nominating committee in their work.
These job descriptions often include Bible references,
role expectations, and function statements.

Bible References.—A popular reference is Psalm
84:10:

> For a day in thy courts is better than a thousand.
> I had rather be a doorkeeper in the house of my
> God, than to dwell in the tents of wickedness.

Some churches who use women ushers point to
2 Samuel 4:6 (RSV). The context of the verse doesn't
place the woman in the Temple; rather, the emphasis
is on her role as a doorkeeper. The same Hebrew
word is used for doorkeeper in both Psalm 84:10 and
2 Samuel 4:6. Apparently the roles were similar in
nature, but the functions were different.

The idea of doorkeeper (porter) carries over into
the New Testament. The key passages are Mark 13:34,
John 10:3, and John 18:15-17. Again these passages
point to what the individual is doing (function) rather
than who the individual is (role).

Another Bible phrase written into some job descriptions for ushers is from Paul's advice to the
Corinthians. "Let all things be done decently and in

order" (1 Cor. 14:40). Paul's emphasis is on worship. He is hopeful that the Christians will remember their purpose for being together. Spontaneity may need to be a part of worship, but it should not be distasteful or distracting. Paul's advice is also good for ushers to remember.

Other phrases, verses, and passages related to love, kindness, helpfulness, and hospitality are too numerous to list but should be remembered.

Role Expectations.—As you might guess, before you were selected to be an usher, someone on the nominating committee probably asked, "What exactly does our church expect an usher to be and to do?" There is a very close relationship between "being" and "doing" for the usher. Let's examine the "being" part first.

I asked the question in an usher training session, "What do the church members and visitors expect from you?" One man said, "They want us to greet them with a smile and seat them on the aisle!" Another person commented, "Don't be in the way but don't go away." An experienced usher told me, "I'm a greeter, meeter, and seater."

If the last responder had added "helper" to his list, he would have named basically what others expect from you as an usher.

You are expected to be a *greeter*. You are on the front line of duty for your church. Many times you are the first impression others have of your church. A friend of mine is fond of saying, "You never have a second chance to make a good first impression." Keep that in mind as you smile and extend your hand to greet a visitor. The same warm smile and firm hand-shake you offer a visitor needs to be extended to all you greet.

You are expected to be a *meeter*. Greeting is a way of saying welcome. Meeting is a way of saying to another person, "You are important; I have time for you."

Your role as a meeter will require some practice. What you say and don't say is always important. There is the right way and the wrong way to meet a person. We will consider in detail some of these matters in chapter 4. For the time being, however, remember that you are expected to be more than a greeter. You must take the next important step and become a skilled meeter.

You are expected to be a *seater*. As with your role of meeter, being a seater is more involved than you may realize. A little later in the book you will learn the "how to" of seating.

Ask any experienced usher for a most embarrassing moment, and I suspect it relates to seating someone. No matter how well you train, how much you practice, you are always in danger of making mistakes in seating. One example will make the point for now. Mr. Smith has been an usher in Central Church for years. He has seated people in the front of the church, in the middle, and in the back all those years.

This fine Sunday morning Mrs. Jones comes for help in finding a seat near the front where she can hear "what's going on." Mrs. Jones is late, as usual, but Usher Smith is kind and leads the way to the front of the church. Mrs. Jones spots a friend and quietly makes her way to a middle area pew.

Unaware of what has happened, Usher Smith is now at the third pew from the front, leaning over and requesting a visitor to slip over and make room for Sister Jones. He turns to guide Mrs. Jones to her seat. Surprise—Mrs. Jones is nowhere to be found.

Usher Smith has created such a disturbance that heads begin to turn, the preacher stutters in the middle of his welcome to the visitors, and nearby children giggle. Usher Smith quickly retreats from the scene, trying to blend into the red carpet. Needless to say, being a seater can be tricky.

You are expected to be a *helper*. Simply stated, you are expected to be ready to handle all emergencies. Emergencies come in all sizes and shapes. To paraphrase a well-known TV show's opening line— "When you least expect it, someone will come up to you and say, 'I have an emergency!'" In chapter 6 we will deal with emergencies—both big and small.

You will need to use standard procedures worked out to handle various situations and good common sense in your role as helper. Remember right now that the folk at the church will look to you for a quick response when emergencies arise.

Well, there you have it—your role as an usher. Are you ready and willing to be a greeter, meeter, seater, and helper?

Function Statements.—You just finished exploring your role—what others expect or perhaps what is written in a job description. Now, you need to consider how to do what is expected. Here's where you put your own personality into your role.

If you examine your role expectations and your functions as an usher, you will discover that the two overlap. You are expected to be a greeter, and you greet. Your job description states that you are a seater, and you function by seating people.

A list of function statements could be noted for each role expectation in your job description. However, the list could only be general in nature. Here are some typical statements (sometime called duties) found in many usher job descriptions:

1. The usher will greet all visitors with a smile.
2. The usher will be prepared to hand out visitors' cards at the appropriate time.
3. The usher will seat worshipers at the appropriate points in the services (check the church bulletin).
4. The usher will aid the pastor and staff during the worship service as needed.
5. The usher will distribute church bulletins and other handouts.
6. The usher will be prepared to handle emergencies.
7. The usher will turn off all lights and regulate the temperature after each service conducted in the sanctuary.

Your specific functions are carried out as you interpret them through your own personality. An example may help. As a greeter, you are encouraged to smile as people arrive or pass near you. No list or no person can tell you how big your smile needs to be or how long you should smile. Your smile is determined by your personality and the specific situation. The same principle can be applied to all the functions of your job. In chapters 3—5 you can examine the general functions of your role as usher.

A factor related to what you do and how you perform your functions is often overlooked. That factor is attitude. Attitude changes like the weather. In fact, the weather may help determine, in part, what your attitude is or is not on various occasions. Remember the last time it rained and you were expecting a sunny day? Somehow the darkness of the sky cast a dark cloud over you, and your attitude was not as cheerful as usual.

Attitude is a matter you need to work on all the time. Attitude affects your performance as an usher. Events will happen to you as you go about your duties that will cause rather sudden attitude swings. If you are prepared, you can keep a positive attitude no matter what happens.

Remember Usher Smith and Mrs. Jones? Usher Smith was embarrassed, and his attitude could have changed for the rest of the service. In fact, he might even have confronted Mrs. Jones about the matter after the worship service.

Or, he might just have said to his fellow ushers, "That was an embarrassing experience, but I'll know next time to keep Mrs. Jones in sight." He learned from what he had experienced and was able to keep his attitude positive.

This chapter began with an illustration. Picture the

same scene again. This time actions of the usher will be included. As you read, take note of the various attitudes expressed by the usher. Usher Cook is our actor.

Usher Cook watches the young couple and baby through the window next to the front door of the church. As they make their way to the front steps, Usher Cook swings the front door open and greets them with a smile.

"Good morning and welcome to our church." Usher Cook extends his hand to the young father and says, "My name is Ron Cook."

"Hi, I'm John Harris, and this is my wife, Alice, and our son, Tim."

"Well, John and Alice," responds Usher Cook, "I'm glad you came to worship with us this morning. Is this your first visit to our church?"

"Yes, we moved into the Lakeview Apartments last weekend and one of your members, Ann Wilson, invited us to come this morning."

"Ann told me you might be coming this morning and to be on the lookout for you. In fact, she has places saved for you in the sanctuary."

During the brief conversation, Alice removes a thin blanket from around Tim and brushed his hair to one side.

"Ann was right," observes Usher Cook, "Tim does have a full head of red hair."

Usher Cook hands John a church bulletin and indicates that the first hymn is about to begin. Turning to Alice to give her a bulletin, Usher Cook notices that Tim's restlessness is demanding Alice's full attention.

"Alice," suggests Usher Cook, "perhaps you'd like to take Tim to stay in our nursery while you and John are in the worship service?"

"No, I believe he'll be all right in a few minutes. Thanks anyway. If he gets too fussy, I'll just bring him out of the service."

"Fine. Let's locate Ann. She'll be happy to see you."

Usher Cook moves ahead of John, Alice, and Tim and opens the sanctuary door; he motions them to follow him into the sanctuary. The congregation is standing and singing a hymn.

Usher Cook locates Ann Wilson and makes eye contact with her. Turning his head in the direction of the Harrises standing in the aisle, Usher Cook whispers to Ann, "Here are the Harrises." Being assured that the Harrises are properly located, Usher Cook makes his way quickly back to his station prepared for whatever happens next.

We have examined only a brief segment of one Sunday morning in the life of Usher Cook. However, enough happened in the segment to illustrate that attitude is important. What did Usher Cook do that was positive? What clues do you have to describe his overall attitude?

Your church believes you have the qualities necessary to serve as an usher. The members of the church feel comfortable with you. They have confidence in your abilities. They will count on you to handle every situation and represent them as the first line of contact the church has with a visitor.

Consider the Responsibilities

Perhaps a member of the church's nominating committee, the head usher, or another person invited you to consider being a church usher. Maybe you were handed a paper listing the duties and responsibilities of an usher. Maybe the duties and responsibilities were given to you verbally. In either case, the list spelled out what was expected.

Now, the responsibility is yours. Can you accept the role others expect of you as a church usher? Can you function as others expect? Can you be responsible for

- greeting members and visitors with a smile and making them feel welcome;
- meeting members and visitors in such a way that they know you are sincere and interested in them;
- seating members and visitors politely, courteously, and in a mannerly fashion;
- helping members and visitors in a quick and confident way with emergencies?

Obviously, there are more details to the responsibilities you will have as an usher. These will be considered carefully in chapters 3—5. However, all of your responsibilities will fall within the broad areas of greeting, meeting, seating, and helping.

Saying yes to the church's invitation to serve as an usher is a major commitment. Don't take the opportunity lightly. You are committing to your church your time to study your responsibilities, time to train for them, time to perform them, and time to evaluate them.

Time to Study.—Every usher, new or experienced, needs to study the responsibilities assigned to the position. At times, responsibilities may be added or deleted. A part of what you are doing by reading this book is studying the role and function of your job.

When you visit other churches on vacation, you will find yourself studying what other ushers are doing. You will observe responsibilities given to other ushers which are similar and different from your own. Learn all you can as you study. Share what you learn with your fellow ushers.

Time to Train.—Most churches will provide opportunities for usher training. If you are a new usher, train all you can before you're called to duty. The experienced usher can benefit from training by sharpening needed skills. There is no substitute for proper training.

Time to Perform.—You may be a member of a church that has a large group of ushers. You are called on to serve on a regular basis but not each Sunday. Or you may be an usher in a smaller church where your services are required every Sunday.

Some churches require their ushers to assist anytime there is a large group using the sanctuary. So the actual time required to perform could be substantial and needs to be considered carefully before you commit to being an usher. If you agree to accept the role and responsibilities, be dependable and available when it's your turn to serve.

Time to Evaluate.—You may have seen the poster that displays the following message: THE SEVEN LAST WORDS OF THE CHURCH—We Never Did It

That Way Before. The truth of the message is evident. Without the option to try something new, death is at the doorstep. Change is possible only when the present is evaluated.

Here's an example: The ushers at Central Church wear a flower as a sign of identification for members and visitors. One Sunday morning the members of a community organization came to Central Church wearing flowers just like the ushers. The pastor, while making his usual greeting to the visitors, indicated that if any in the congregation needed help during or after the service, an usher was prepared to help. "You can easily spot the ushers. They are wearing a flower," advised the pastor. You see the problem.

After a discussion of the confusion caused by the flowers, Central Church ushers can now be identified by the flower they wear and the satin ribbon that displays the word *usher*.

Evaluation can be done on the spot to correct a situation. Evaluation can be done on a regular basis as a part of regular usher meetings.

Self-evaluation is an activity you owe to yourself regularly to determine whether you are measuring up to what is expected of you by the church and what you expect of yourself. You have the responsibility to evaluate—who you are as an usher and what you are doing in that role.

Trained for Service

Interviews with experienced ushers reveal both positive and negative attitudes about their places of service in the church. They comment about good times and bad times. They point to experiences of joy and times of embarrassment. A key factor that kept surfacing for these ushers was training—mostly the lack of it. There appears to be some relationship between positive attitudes, good times, joyous experiences, and training.

Proper training gives you a positive mind-set to perform a task you are about to undertake. Training cuts down on fears. Recall for a moment how you learned to swim. Did someone push you into the water and laugh as you struggled to stay afloat? Or did someone take the time to explain the principles of swimming and then go into the water with you?

Swimming and ushering are similar at the point of training. Training, if properly done, will prepare you for many wonderful experiences and help you develop a positive attitude as you begin your service to the Lord and the church.

Hopefully, you are reading this book in preparation for some training sessions. Your church wants you properly trained and prepared. If, however, you are reading for information only, consider this as an opportunity for training. The activities in "Usher Training Helps" in the back of the book will aid you as you consider all phases of your role and functions.

Training on your own or in a group process is developed in three stages: the initial stage, the on-the-job stage, and the questioning stage.

Initial Stage.—This is the introductory time of training. You begin to notice the active ushers at your church. You study their moves and note the way they do things. You anticipate what you will do when you become an active usher.

The head usher may call or visit with you and describe your responsibilities. He may share an assignment sheet indicating when you are to serve. He may give you material to study. He may share with you this book.

Another part of the initial stage may involve you in a series of training sessions. The head usher or a number of the experienced ushers may be asked to discuss with you your role and responsibilities. You may spend time in practice sessions going over the details of your tasks.

The pastor and staff may attend the training sessions and share their expectations of you as a new usher. Be a good student and learn all you can during this initial stage.

On-the-Job Stage.—Some new ushers are assigned to more experienced ushers for a period of time. This procedure allows you, as a new usher, to learn by observation. You follow the lead of the experienced usher. You are taken step-by-step through your responsibilities. The "butterflies" you may experience on the first Sunday you serve will be fewer because you can count on the guidance of the experienced usher. The unexpected questions from a visitor or the request of a member can be directed to the experienced usher. You can observe, listen, and learn.

Confusion often occurs when a new usher is "thrown into the water" and told to perform. True, you may learn on the job; but you may also decide that ushering is more than you expected and that you're not really ready for the challenge. Hopefully, you will say, "I need some training!"

On-the-job training allows you to practice. You develop confidence in your abilities. You begin to add your own personality to your duties. You develop your own style.

Many experienced ushers comment that they still value the things they learned and the help they received from on-the-job training. By the way, the same ushers keep their eyes and ears open each time they serve. There is always something to learn if you're open to the opportunities around you.

Questioning Stage.—This stage of your training is very important. As a new usher, you will have questions galore. Your practice and on-the-job experiences will answer many of your questions. However, never hesitate to ask questions about any phases of your responsibilities. The head usher or a more experienced usher will have an answer or can find an answer to your question. Answers will give you information; and the more information you have, the better you can carry out your responsibilities.

Ed White was a new usher and was recognized as something of a hero by the church members. Earlier in the year Ed responded to a need and was able to help because he had the needed information.

During a training session Ed had posed the question, "This may sound silly, but do we have responsibility for the parking lot on Sunday morning?"

"Yes, we do," the smiling head usher Dixon responded, "but we count on the members to park their own cars."

Usher White was conscientious and eager to do a good job as a new usher. Each time he opened the front door to greet a person he glanced in the general direction of the parking lot. On one of these occasions he noticed a large puff of dark smoke coming from the hood of a car.

As he neared the car, it was apparent the car was on fire. He moved quickly to help the members of the family out of the burning car. By that time, others had arrived to extinguish the fire. A question, an answer, and a reaction prevented a tragedy.

Ask all the questions you need to. The answers may be useful the next time you serve.

Training is important to you as you begin a new career as a church usher. Training is important for the experienced usher as skills are constantly in need of upgrading. To be the very best at what you do—train.

Your Place to Serve

Being selected as an usher and being trained to fill the role and carry out the functions of an usher are only two-thirds of actually serving as an usher. Your response is required to unite the fractions into a whole. Without your willingness to serve, the selecting and the training mean very little.

Years ago when a person gave his word on a matter, you could count on its being his bond. In fact, you've probably heard it said: "His word is his bond." The same should be true for you in your acceptance to serve as an usher. You are saying to your church, "You can count on me."

You will be able to honor the trust the church has placed in you by being the best usher possible. They have provided you a place to serve; now, it's your opportunity to serve. Determine right now that dependability will be the trademark of your service as an usher. Be in your assigned place ready to serve.

Should it be necessary for you to miss an assigned Sunday, contact the head usher as soon as possible. Be dependable! If a training session or evaluation session is scheduled for ushers, attend. Be dependable!

The more years you serve as an usher, the more opportunities will come your way to learn, encourage, and witness. Working with people will become a high interest in your life.

Opportunity to Learn.—Training and practice will help you learn and master the art of greeting, meeting, seating, and helping others in your church. A major by-product of your service will be the new people skills you learn and develop. You will begin to put names and faces together. You will take pride in learning and recalling names. You will enjoy introducing people—visitors to members and visitors to visitors. You will learn to be a people person in your concern, actions, and love.

Opportunities to Encourage.—An outgrowth of your love for people will be your positive efforts to encourage them. You will find ways to make the members and visitors glad they are in God's house. Your warm

smile and personal words will bring sunshine and joy
to many. Some members will make it a point to seek
you out, shake your hand, and give you a personal
greeting because you have taken the time to encourage them in the past.

Your fellow ushers can be a target of your encour-
agement. An extra pat on the back for a job well done
can be your way of saying, "You are doing a good job.
I appreciate you." A personal note or telephone call
from you to a fellow usher who is out sick will show
your support and concern.

You will foster good feelings among the members
and visitors when you look for and take opportunities
to encourage.

Opportunity to Witness.—Your service as an usher
will place you in a strategic location to witness. You
will have the opportunity to show the love of Christ
as you interact with members and visitors. Your
mood will be caught by many who are entering the
sanctuary for worship. A positive mood will help
them be positive.

An older gentleman, who had been an usher for
years, suggested to a group of new ushers that they
offer a witness phrase with their greetings. His favorites were: "Good morning, Jesus loves you." "Greetings. This is the day the Lord has made." "Smile,
Jesus loves you, and I love you." His point was to
plant a positive word about Jesus and allow the Holy
Spirit to use it during the service.

You will have opportunities for witnessing. Be
ready to share your faith.

Someone has commented, "Anything worth doing is worth doing well." Take that to heart. Put it into practice as you usher. Ushering is worth doing. So do it well.

2
What Every Usher Needs

If you had the power to create the perfect church usher, what qualities would you include? The qualities available are almost endless. No doubt when you completed your task and gave the usher a place to serve, you would be pleased. Or would you?

Just suppose your usher is serving and you are observing. All is going great. Your usher is friendly to the church members and visitors. Members are being seated properly. Visitors are being made to feel welcome. The worship service is beginning.

All of a sudden you hear your usher laugh. The laughter becomes louder and uncontrolled. Well, you think about the qualities you gave your usher. Humor is surely one of the qualities you included. Every usher needs a sense of humor. You notice also that members of the congregation are turning around to look at your usher.

The minister and members of the choir are looking around searching for the source of the loud, uncontrolled laughter. Then you realize: You forgot to give your usher a sense of reverence. You assumed every usher would have a sense of reverence built in. You goofed, but it's all right. There is no perfect church usher, and this was a made-up situation after all.

The point is that you, as a church usher, have a great number of positive qualities already. At the same time, you need to realize there are qualities you can develop.

In this chapter a number of qualities will be listed and described. You will find qualities you already possess. Hopefully, you will discover qualities you can develop.

Let's consider the qualities in three groups: qualities you can't do without; qualities you may need to develop; and qualities others expect you to have. Many of the same qualities could be listed in any of the groups. That means those qualities are doubly important—to you and to others.

Qualities You Can't Do Without

Self-introspection is not an ego trip. It's an honest effort on your part to know yourself—what you think and how you feel. In this case its purpose is to examine the qualities you possess that you use every day of your life. You bring those same qualities to your service as a church usher. You don't separate the qualities you have by the days of the week—some for Sunday; others for the weekdays. You are what you are. But there's always room for improvement. Let's explore some qualities you can't do without.

A Good Self-Image.—What you feel about yourself is important. Learn to live with yourself. Learn to laugh at yourself. Don't take yourself too seriously. Accept yourself as human and not superhuman. You will make mistakes as an usher. Learn from your mistakes, but don't punish yourself. If you are down on yourself, it will show in how you perform.

You are in control of your self-image. You determine your feelings about you. True, many external forces come into play that affect your feelings. But even with those forces, you determine how they are processed. If your self-image is good, you can process negative forces created by others. If you don't properly process negative forces, your self-image suffers.

To illustrate this important point, consider the following: It's Sunday morning and you're meeting and greeting members and visitors as they enter the church building. Mrs. Wilson, a church member, introduces her special friend Mrs. Smyth. Your response is: "Mrs. Smith, I'm glad . . . "

Before you can complete your statement, Mrs. Wilson has jumped in and says, "I said Smyth, not Smith. It's S-M-Y-T-H!" The brief scene creates enough disturbance that others turn to see and hear. Mrs. Wilson and her friend move on into the sanctuary.

When a scene like that takes place, a number of things happen. First, instant embarrassment is created because you made a mistake. You repeated the name you thought you heard. Second, you are totally involved in a scene that's out of control. Nothing you say will really please Mrs. Wilson. Third, the mistake and scene will have carry-over effect. You will greet Mrs. Wilson again.

Now, let's examine your self-image in terms of the scene with Mrs. Wilson. There are at least two thoughts you could have about it. "I goofed," is one thought, "but I will do better next time." That's positive for your self-image. A second thought is, "I goofed, and maybe I'll goof up every time. Maybe I don't have what it takes to be an usher."

That's negative for your self-image. If you allow too many negative forces to go unprocessed, you begin to question all your skills and abilities; and your self-image will become negative. As the song says, "You've got to accentuate the positive and eliminate the negative."

Many of your experiences will create self-doubt and cause you to question your abilities. However, look for the positive factor in each experience, and learn to feel good about yourself and your developing skills.

A Good Sense of Humor.—This quality does not mean that you must have a bag full of jokes ready to use at any moment. Nor does it mean that you need to be the good humor comic of the ushers. However, it does mean that you need to know when humor is appropriate. You must learn to sense the need for humor. Some situations that develop at church demand humor. Other situations are just as strong in not requiring humor.

It seems appropriate to define the word *humor*. According to Webster, humor is "a sudden, unpredictable, or unreasoning inclination" or "something that is or is designed to be comical or amusing."

In terms of the definition, humor appears to be suitable in most situations. Yet there are times when humor may not be appropriate at the church. Consider the following:

- The first encounter with a visitor. (The visitor's response to your greeting may indicate he is open to humor.)
- Handling emergencies.
- Ushering for a special occasion such as a funeral.
- Dealing with folk who do not respond to your brand of humor.
- When responding to a serious request.

There may be other items you can add to the list. That's what you should do. Create your own list.

Most situations and people are open to humor. However, your humor needs to be a natural part of your personality and always positive. Ethnic, sexual, vulgar, degrading forms of humor have no place in church (or any other place). As long as you work with people, a good sense of humor is a quality you can't do without.

A Good Appearance.—After visitors have entered the church building, you are the first person they encounter. Your appearance will impress or depress them and may well set the tone for their experience at church that day. A little time spent in checking your appearance may be the difference between a positive or negative impression. Your final check could be the last thing you do before you leave home or the first activity you do at church. A quick once-over, head to toe, is needed. Here's a checklist:

- Hair. Is it combed/brushed? Do you need a cut or trim?
- Face. Is your face neatly groomed? Could any part of your face call negative attention to

itself? If you are ushering at night, be sure to groom again before the evening service.

- Hands. Are they clean? How much jewelry do they display? Too much hand jewelry could create problems when shaking hands. Check your nails. Are they clean? If you wear them long, are they attractive?

- Jewelry. In addition to the hands, jewelry may be worn to adorn other parts of the body. A general rule for jewelry is: if it calls attention to itself, it's too much.

- Clothing. Is it clean? Is it appropriate? Clothing can be contemporary and fashionable and yet not call special attention to the wearer. If you have a problem with color blindness, ask someone to help with this part of your checking. Is all underclothing hidden from view?

- Shoes. Are they clean? Funny as it may sound, do they match? If you have walked through a grassy area at your home or on the church grounds, give your shoes a special check.

The seasons of the year also need to be remembered when a good appearance is important. During the warm months, your usher group may decide to dress for the warmer temperatures. You may shed your coats and agree to go in short sleeves.

It's best to have some uniformity in appearance for all the usher group. Rolled-up long sleeves will look out of place if all of the other ushers are in short sleeves. The point is this: Plan your appearance to ensure that it does not distract others. If distractions are allowed to creep in, your efforts will be lessened and your effectiveness reduced.

Good Personal Hygiene.—Avoid being avoided! If church members appear to intentionally avoid you, check your personal hygiene. Sometimes even your best friend will not tell you that you have a hygiene problem which is offensive. Just like your appearance, your personal hygiene needs a check. Here are some areas for concern:

- Hair. Check for dandruff. Take special notice if you are wearing a dark garment. You need to discover and solve the dandruff problem before you hear others talking and you are the subject of the conversation.

  Styled or unstyled hair needs to be clean and neat.

- Face. Beards and mustaches are very popular. They should be cared for in the same way as hair—clean and neat in appearance. Years ago nothing needed to be said about cosmetics. However, today cosmetics are available for both sexes. Complexion items can be used by both sexes. Either a light or a heavy use of cosmetics needs to be done with taste.

- Shoulders. Dandruff lands on shoulders and so does loose hair. If your custom is to comb or brush your hair just prior to your ushering responsibilities, take the time to give your shoulders a look.

- Breath. If you have ever been on the receiving end of a bad breath blast, you realize how offensive this element of hygiene can be.

Nearly everything you put in your mouth has the potential for causing bad breath. Food items, drinks, tobacco, medicine—all contribute to bad breath.

What can help the problem? Well, keeping your teeth and mouth clean will help. Some folk even suggest scrubbing your tongue periodically. Also try mouthwash, breath mints, breath sprays, and chewing gum (not while you're serving, please). Choose one that meets your needs.

- Body Odor. Good personal hygiene requires proper care of your body. Daily cleaning of the body is a must. Special care needs to be taken to clean those parts of the body that tend to produce odor. Application of body powders, lotions, and deodorants should be used as appropriate.

Care needs to be taken not to overdo a good thing. Too much "good smelling stuff" (perfume, cologne, after-shave, and the like) is nearly as bad as too little. Use the amount needed to do the job, but don't go to extremes.

A clean body deserves clean clothes—from the inside to the outside. Garments have a way of absorbing body perspiration. It does not take an expert to determine when a garment needs cleaning. Make sure you check often.

- Shoes. Shoes can be offensive if care is not taken. They can pick up foreign matter such

WHAT EVERY USHER NEEDS   **39**

as animal excretion, gasoline, garbage, and
so forth. All of these can create odor problems (often credited to you by mistake) if left
unchecked.

No usher wants to develop a bad reputation due to
bad personal hygiene. Avoid being avoided—check
your personal hygiene!

A Love for People.—When it comes to loving people,
Jesus is a perfect model for you. Jesus loved people of
all ages, in all situations, at all stations of life, with no
questions asked. You need to have a love for people
that is blind to color, age, sex, position, importance,
appearance, or any other factor that creates barriers.

On any given Sunday you will encounter a variety
of people. Some you will have known for years;
others you will meet for the first time. All that you
meet need to sense your love and concern for them by
your actions and your words. A warm smile, a firm
handshake, a personal word should be automatic
actions on your part. Be mindful that Jesus said,
"Verily I say unto you, Inasmuch as ye have done it
unto one of the least of these my brethren, ye have
done it unto me" (Matt. 25:40).

As much as is within you, your love for people
needs to be consistent. A young adult shared before
the congregation one evening what Mr. Collins, an
usher, meant to him: "Some of my earliest childhood
memories of church are of shaking hands with Mr.
Collins at the front door of this building. I never
remember a time when he was not there smiling and
shaking hands with those who came his way. He
never had to say the words, but I knew then and I

know now that Mr. Collins loves me." This was a fine tribute to a church usher who found joy in loving people in the name of Jesus Christ.

A Sense of Reverence.—Some folk have the idea that church is the place to be quiet and put on a long face. They also associate this attitude with reverence. You must learn to balance a need for reverence in God's house with a thought from King David, who wrote, "I was glad when they said unto me,/Let us go into the house of the Lord" (Ps. 122:1).

Like humor, you must have a sense of reverence. There are actions that nearly everyone would identify as lacking in reverence. The same action in a different situation would be quite acceptable. Take, for example, Usher Watkins and his habit of whistling.

He whistles at home, on the job—nearly everyplace. He whistles because he's happy and does so almost unconsciously. Usher Watkins must guard himself against whistling in the sanctuary because that activity does not seem to present appropriate respect and honor to God. Usher Watkins has a sense of reverence.

The standards for reverence are usually set by the local congregation. You will pick up these standards as a church member. Then when you serve as an usher, you will become even more conscious of observing them.

Prayer is a good way to illustrate this. In some congregations when prayer is made, only the person praying can be heard. In other congregations members feel that it's appropriate to respond to words and phrases they hear in the prayer. Other church groups consider it quite acceptable to have a number of members praying aloud simultaneously. Reverence through prayer would be defined differently by each church group. Yet, by their own standards, each is showing reverence. Your task is to understand your local situation and be an example for members and visitors as they seek to express reverence. Your actions and attitude of reverence will be a model to others.

Let's move now to consider some qualities you may not recognize in yourself.

Qualities You May Need to Develop

The world-famous Hope Diamond is on display at a Washington, D.C. museum. As a person views this masterpiece, he is aware of its uniqueness. Yet its current status is the work of nature and man. Nature took many years to create the rough stone. An expert diamond cutter had to study, cut, and polish the stone to give it its current shape. Without proper development, the Hope Diamond would not exist.

That's the way it is with your personal qualities. Some of your qualities are evident and used all the time. Other attributes, like an undeveloped diamond, are within you but are still "in the rough" and need to be polished. Those are the ones we will consider in this section.

A Willingness to Learn.—Some strange attitudes exist related to the actual work of an usher. Too often folk accept the position of usher by reasoning, "I don't want to teach a class at church because that requires a lot of study time. But I'll be glad to usher once a month because anyone can do that."

The chairman of the church nominating committee may say, "Let's keep a list of the folk who are unwilling to serve as leaders and ask them to be ushers." In both cases the attitudes about ushers are questionable.

You know the functions and responsibilities of an usher are demanding. Ushers are leaders of the first order and not just "anyone can do" the work of an usher. It takes years of dedication, training, and practice to master all that is required of an usher. Therefore, an usher, new or experienced, must be willing to learn.

A large downtown church found it necessary, for safety reasons, to install a surveillance system. The system required a camera at each entrance and a centrally controlled door-lock trip for some of the entrances. The control center was a mass of switches, buttons, and video screens. The ushers had the responsibility of learning and operating the system. Extensive training was required for each usher to properly perform the task.

With the coming of the electronic age to the church, most ushers will be expected to take on new tasks requiring additional training. If you are unwilling to learn, you may find yourself limited in your service. You develop the quality of a willingness to learn by being open and constantly asking the question, "What can I learn today that will make me a better usher?"

A Good Memory.—Memory is a quality most people have to develop. Few are born with a natural ability for remembering. Memory for you as an usher comes in a number of ways. Part of your memory is developed as a result of practice. Seating folk is an activity you do over and over each Sunday. You don't stop to think about the proper seating technique to use; it's automatic. You remember the steps in the process.

Wouldn't it be nice if everything you had to remember came as automatically as seating folk in a pew? Unfortunately, some activities where memory is required are not automatic. Those require work, practice, and patience.

A major memory activity you face each Sunday is remembering names and relationships. If you usher in a small church, remembering names may not be a major concern. You probably have grown up in the church and have known most of the people for a while. You still must add to your memory the names of those who visit and new members.

But adding a few names a week to your memory should not be difficult. A more pressing concern for you is remembering relationships. Quite often in a smaller congregation families intermarry and family relationships become very important. You will need to make every effort to keep family relationships clear.

If you usher in a large church, keeping family relationships clear may not be as important as trying to keep up with the names of new members and frequent visitors.

There are a lot of "improve your memory" books on the market. Most of the books point to three basic principles for developing a better memory. These same principles can apply to you no matter what size church you serve.

- Concentrate. When you are introduced to a person for the first time, concentrate on the name you hear. If you don't hear the name or you hear only part of the name, ask that the name be repeated. Repeat the name back quickly. In fact, try to use the name a number of times in the conversation.

- Associate. When you hear a name for the first time, associate it with another person you know quite well. Standing before you is a visitor, Mr. Grant. You already know a fellow at work named Bill Grant. Create a mental picture of the visitor standing alongside Bill Grant. Get the idea?

  Sometimes you may need to associate a new name with an object. Suppose you are introduced to Mr. Potts. Create a mental picture of Mr. Potts and a special flower pot you have at home. If you need to, mentally picture Mr. Potts with the special flower pot on his head. The next time you see Mr. Potts a mental picture should flash through your mind. The more you practice, the easier this activity becomes.

- Practice. No matter what system you devise to improve your memory, you will need to practice. You meet a new person on Sunday morning. That night you see the person at church again. Repeat the person's name mentally. You may see this person later in the week at a shopping center. Repeat his name mentally. Greet him and say his name if the situation is appropriate. Practice.

Work on your memory. You will be pleased with the results.

A Sense of Tact.—Tact is knowing what to do or say in an effort to maintain good relations. You may already have this ability to some extent; but you will agree, there's always room for improvement.

An informal survey of church members suggests that some of the flare-ups that happen at church could have been prevented if the individuals involved had been more tactful. You may be caught in the middle of a flare-up. Some situation, not of your making, will require a great measure of tact on your part.

Have you noticed that some church members sit in the same pew each time? The Green family is that way. They have occupied the sixth pew, left side, for as long as anyone can remember. No regular church member would dare sit in the Greens' pew for Sunday morning worship.

That is, not until a new family comes in early one Sunday and breaks the long-standing tradition. It's your happy privilege to usher the Greens to another pew. This situation could be explosive unless you are able to defuse it calmly. That's called tact.

Being tactful in most cases requires that you size up a situation quickly, determine possible alternatives, speak and act in Christian love, and be calm.

Let's see how the formula could work with the Greens. As you lead the Greens down the aisle, you see that their regular pew is taken. You may suggest another pew nearby or, if time permits, introduce the Greens to the new family and suggest they sit together and visit prior to the service.

Sometimes your tact will be effective and at times it won't. In either case, practice and experience will help you develop this needed quality. Be open to the suggestions of others as you develop. Your positive response to constructive criticism may be a major development in your tactfulness.

A Sense of Timing.—Timing is the ability to take appropriate action which leads to a positive result. Timing can be verbal or nonverbal depending on the situation.

Timing is a twin of tact. These qualities work together and often are developed together. One helps the other.

There are situations in your ushering experiences when proper timing is a must. You can develop a sense of timing that will help you, your fellow church members, visitors, and other ushers with whom you serve.

Timing may be as simple as opening a door for a new mother who has her arms full with her new baby, a diaper bag, her Bible, and her purse. Or timing may be as complex as preventing a fight between two teenage boys.

Both extremes require a sense of timing. Appropriate action on your part should have positive results. Here are a few factors to consider as you work to develop a sense of timing:

- Be alert to what's happening around you.

- Look and listen for clues that can move you into action.
- Take the initiative when appropriate and needed.
- Study and analyze the timing of other ushers.
- Anticipate the verbal and nonverbal actions of others.
- Trust your intuition.
- Learn from your timing mistakes.

A Helpful Attitude.—This quality could easily be listed as "going the second mile." Some ushers read an usher job description and seldom vary from it. They try to accomplish what is written in the description to the best of their ability. That's good. However, no job description can detail every act of helpfulness required of you. That's why you need to develop a helpful attitude.

A helpful attitude is one that looks for opportunities over and above the routine actions and experiences that are shared with other individuals. It's as Jesus said to his followers in the Sermon on the Mount, "Whosoever shall compel thee to go a mile, go with him twain" (Matt. 5:41).

There's an element of surprise in the action of "going the second mile." The action says something about you as a person, but it says volumes when you act in the name of the Lord.

Don't develop this quality to receive praise of men. Helpfulness is an attitude you seek to develop because you recognize people are important, and you can have a part in their lives through positive action.

Let's turn our attention to the last group of qualities. Your opportunity for service is greater when you
know what others expect of you.

Qualities Others Expect You to Have

You have been selected to serve as an usher because
you possess a number of good personal qualities.
Someone has probably said of you, "I think he would
make a good usher. He needs to be considered the
next time ushers are chosen." Although no qualities
are mentioned, the statements presume that you have
exhibited noticeable positive qualities which have
been remembered.

It's normal for different church members to expect
different qualities in you. Church members will have
different needs and concerns at varying times and
will look to you for help. However, there are some
general qualities most church members (and at times
visitors) want all ushers to have. These are very self-
evident, yet need to be mentioned.

A Dedication to the Task.—Whatever method was
used to select you as an usher, someone had confidence in your abilities and recognized potential in
your qualities. The congregation expects you to be
dedicated to your usher responsibilities. They want
you to mature as an usher and do the very best you
can. And you will, if you are dedicated to the task.

A Positive Attitude.—You will make contact with all
sorts of folk and be confronted by a variety of
situations as you usher. Many of these will try your
patience and have a tendency to turn your attitude in
a negative direction. Guard against pessimism.

On any given Sunday you may influence others to be optimistic. Your smile, greetings, and warmth will be caught by others. The congregation expects you to have a consistently positive outlook. Don't disappoint them.

A Courteous Manner.—The congregation is eager for visitors to feel welcome when they come. The pastor and staff count on you to be courteous in all matters. There are times when a situation calls for very strong directive action. It's especially important to maintain a courteous manner at all times. You are on the front line, and the impression you make is momentous.

Your courteous manner will be evident to others through your thoughtfulness, graciousness, attentiveness, politeness, gentleness, and personal attention.

A Personal Calmness.—When the emergencies come, big or small, the congregation will expect you to be calm. You must be ready to move into action while keeping your composure. Others will look to you for direction and will count on your ability to handle the situation.

Calmness is a quality that indicates to others, "I can handle this emergency. You can count on me." Your personal calmness may well be the key factor that allows others to be calm when it really counts.

A Christian Witness.—You will recall that the matter of witnessing was mentioned in chapter 1. Witnessing is important in your ushering activities. The congregation expects you to be a positive witness. Other than a brief word of welcome, you may not have extended periods of time to talk with folk about their faith.

But your brief encounter may be the first step in developing a relationship that will give you the time needed later. That's why the qualities mentioned in this chapter are so important. They set the stage, so often, for witnessing opportunities.

Visitors who are not Christians may form an early impression of Christian faith and life-style as a result of being greeted by you. They may recognize qualities in you that express your Christian faith.

You will want to follow up on the contacts you make as an usher. Your church may have a regular follow-up program of evangelism and witnessing. If so, feed your list of contacts into the program. Or follow up personally.

Your Christian witness is a part of your faith commitment to Christ. The congregation expects you to be a positive Christian influence in the lives of all you encounter.

You have examined a lot of qualities in this chapter. Weigh each of them carefully. Allow them to challenge you as you strive to be the very best usher you can be.

3
At Work Before the Worship Service

The concern of this chapter is to highlight those activities you are involved in as an usher prior to the worship service. Specifically, the time frame is about thirty to forty-five minutes. It's that period of time after you arrive at the church building until the hour of worship begins.

Some church groups find it necessary to adjust the time for the worship services. The traditional worship hour is eleven till twelve noon. However, seasonal schedules, special occasions, special emphases, building programs, and other factors may change the time of the worship hour. You will need to read this chapter in terms of your own local situation. However, the time frame is the same, and the activities are basic to all situations.

The key factor related to all that happens prior to the worship hour is preparation. Let's examine four areas of preparation: you, your fellow ushers, your assigned work area, and greeting the people.

Are You Ready?

Ushering is more than just showing up at the church building on Sunday. The congregation expects

more than just a warm body to occupy a space. You need to make some preparation to be ready to usher.

Prepared Physically.—A long, hard Saturday night has a way of leaving telltale signs on a body Sunday morning. The physical part of you responds best when you've had proper rest. A tired body reacts slowly. Drowsiness is a natural response your body makes when rest is needed. You can almost count on an unusual number of yawns when you've not had your regular amount of rest. Yawns come at most inappropriate times—like when you're greeting a visitor.

The cold and flu bugs take their toll on ushers. You may also be a person who suffers from hay fever. All of these ailments are normally accompanied by coughs, sniffles, sneezes, and headaches. You might feel better not ushering when these ailments occur. In that event, the head usher needs to be contacted if you do not feel physically fit to serve.

Here is one last thought related to your physical preparedness. Use your good common sense in knowing when to return to service after you've been out due to illness or an accident. You can indicate your dedication by keeping the head usher aware of your recovery progress.

Physical well-being is so important because it often plays directly into the next phase of preparedness.

Prepared Mentally.—There is a strong relationship between your physically well body and your mentally well body. Quite often the physical part of you places the mental part of you in jeopardy. If you are in pain physically, your mental makeup may be unusually affected.

Usher Gibbs is normally a healthy person. On Friday he fell at work and strained his back. The pain is placing a strain on his normally good nature. Sunday morning Usher Gibbs is not his usual happy self and is overly irritable.

If you can identify with Usher Gibbs, it might be best to request a leave of absence until your physical pain is gone.

Rushing is another matter that strains your mental makeup. Have you noticed "your state of mind" on those occasions when, for one reason or another, everything goes wrong? Usually the slowdowns come when you have a deadline to meet. You try to make up time, become irritated at family members, and arrive at church with your "tongue hanging out."

And in that frame of mind you're ready to usher! If that's your usual routine on Sunday, do yourself and those you may encounter a favor. Work out a personal schedule which allows you to be mentally sharp when you usher.

Mental readiness also shows up as a negative to others if you are daydreaming or preoccupied with a matter. Some folk will question you to determine whether everything is all right if they have been standing nearby while you've been in a trance.

Emotional strain hits everyone. Events in life create problems for your emotions. You know better than anyone about your emotional makeup. If you have recently gone through an emotionally draining experience such as a death in the family, loss of job, or other similar tragedies, you may need some time to recover before you usher. You know already that any given Sunday of ushering may create unusual emotional strain. So protect your emotional health.

Ushering calls for mental and emotional sharpness. Be prepared.

Prepared Socially.—This phase of preparedness relates to the matter of social acceptance. You may want to review the items noted in chapter 2 under "Qualities You Can't Do Without."

You will want to devise and use your own checkup system. If you have a close buddy in the usher group, you may want to form a "check the other person out" system. This allows the other person to look at you objectively and point out areas that need help. If you choose to use this system, understand that comments are made to improve your social acceptance. Do not become defensive.

How you feel physically and mentally also relates to your sociability. Your normally pleasing smile may quickly change to a frown if you are experiencing physical pain or mental stress. A social slipup or miscue may live to haunt you for a number of weeks to come.

It would be much easier to be excused from duty when you are feeling down socially than to sacrifice the good reputation you have worked so hard to attain. You must consider the lasting results of your actions.

Prepared Spiritually.—Some ushering groups meet a few minutes prior to their appointed time for ushering. During this time they discuss any special needs to be handled during the service. They also have a word of Scripture and prayer together. Here's a prayer one usher used in the meeting:

> Father, this is your day and we thank you for sharing it with us. Be with us today as we greet people in your Son's name. Help us in every action we do and every word we say that your name may be glorified. Make us the best ushers possible. Amen.

Circumstances may not allow you and your group to meet. However, you can find time for your own personal spiritual preparation. Select a time at your home or at church when you can shut out the pressures of the moment.

One usher suggested that he uses his car as a quiet place for prayer and spiritual preparation. He drives his family to the front door, parks the car, and has his quiet time.

Use your prayer time to praise God for his goodness. Make your request to the Father for direction and guidance. Be specific with your request. If you are to be involved in a special ushering activity that requires calmness, pray for calmness to properly handle the activity.

If you are not spiritually prepared, negative thoughts have a way of creeping into your life. Too often, the negative thoughts manifest themselves through your attitudes and actions. Then your effective witness and service are hurt and become limited.

Your preparedness to usher begins with a look at

you, but it doesn't stop there. You must become a part of the ushering group.

Are You in the Group?

There may be two, two hundred, or any number in between in your ushering group. The number is not that important, but your relationship to the group is very important. You must learn to cooperate with, trust, and depend on the members of your group. If you are in the group, you owe its members some things. Let's examine a few matters.

Loyalty.—This means you are faithful to the group. Your fellow ushers can count on you to carry out your tasks to the best of your ability. You are in your place of service or you have notified the head usher of your delay or absences. You are on time and you are prepared to serve. You attend planning and training sessions designed for the group.

Courtesy.—The relationship you build with the members of your group is based on Christian love. Your actions and attitudes toward those in your group can be described by the Golden Rule, "Do unto others as you would have them do unto you." Consideration for the well-being of your fellow ushers becomes your guiding principle in developing and maintaining relationships.

Dependability.—This matter has been mentioned a number of times already, but it's worth repeating. You will need to count on the dependability of the other ushers, and they will need to depend on you. Dependability is a mutual benefit for you and your fellow ushers.

If your name is on the schedule to serve, you need to be in your place, on time, prepared to serve. Don't get the reputation of being a no-show. Be dependable.

Supportive.—Your usher group needs only one leader. Every effective group needs a leader, but one too many leaders cuts down on effectiveness.

Give the head usher your full support. Back his efforts to form and maintain an effective and efficient team of ushers.

Be supportive of new ushers. If you are an experienced usher, an encouraging word from you will be a positive stroke for a new usher.

Give your support to each usher on the team. Don't reserve all your smiles and warmth for the church members and visitors. Share yourself with your fellow ushers. What you give away will be returned to you many times over. If you want support, be supportive.

Nonprotective.—At first glance, you may think that being nonprotective is a strange matter to be considered. However, if you will do a quick mental survey, you'll be able to focus on an usher in your group who is very protective of the area he usually occupies.

Some ushers want to be assigned to the same area all the time. They feel confident and comfortable there. Some ushers want to have the freedom to roam. They feel this freedom is necessary. Both wishes are fine, if the entire group feels that's the best and most effective way to get the job done.

In the former approach, be aware that territories can be built and disagreements created when fellow ushers seem to invade established areas. In the latter approach, some areas may be left unattended.

The best way to keep from developing a protective stance is to take turns serving in various areas. No areas are left unattended. The variety makes you and your fellow ushers more valuable because you are not limited to one area. This method also allows the head usher more freedom in planning a work schedule for you and the group.

Before the worship service begins it's vital that you look at yourself, relate to your fellow ushers, and make sure your assigned area is ready.

Is Your Assigned Area Ready?

Many usher groups use some type of checklist to make assignments to each usher. In this way, you know the area and special assignments for which you are responsible. This orderly procedure allows for all areas and assignments to be covered.

On page 60 is an example of a checklist sheet you might be handed. An area floor plan sheet on page 61 may be printed on the back of the checklist or printed separately. These examples fit a church situation requiring the service of six ushers. You will need to translate the two sheets to fit your own local situation.

Consider the two sheets as your assignment for a given Sunday. Both sheets give clear directions for your responsibilities. Remember that the other ushers are depending on you.

Let's translate your sheets into service. Your sheets have your name on them, Usher You. The date for the

Checklist

for Usher _*You*_

_____ (AM) PM
(date)

☑ Serve in Section A—B—(C)—D—E—F

☐ Doors Unlocked

☑ Bulletins in Hand

☑ Visitors Cards Ready (pencils available)

☐ Temperature Set at ____ Degrees

☐ Lights On

☑ Offering Plates Ready

☐ Seat During Worship Service (C)—D—E—F

☐ _____

☐ _____

Special Assignment:

☑ *Reserve pews 2 and 3 in Section 3*

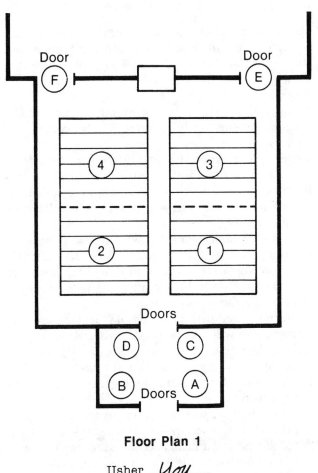

Floor Plan 1

Usher _You_

Date: _____

Service: (AM)–PM

specific worship service and the time (AM or PM) are indicated. You are scheduled to serve in Section C of the vestibule. Notice on the floor plan sheet that Section C is on the right side at the entrance to the sanctuary.

You will be responsible for having a supply of the church bulletins ready to share with members and visitors. You will need to be ready with sufficient visitors' cards when the official welcome is made to the visitors from the pulpit. Your bulletin will indicate the time for this activity. Always review the bulletin to be certain when various activities are scheduled during the service.

In the example being considered, the offering is taken by you and the other ushers. The offering plates are kept on a table in your area of the vestibule. It's your duty to get the offering plates to their proper place before the service begins.

At the scheduled time, usually just before the sermon, you will take your assigned seat during the service. In this case it's seat C (see Floor Plan 2 on page 86). You will give attention to matters in Section 1 and be prepared to act if an emergency should occur in your section.

On the Sunday you are serving, a special group in the church will be given special recognition. You are to see that pews 2 and 3 in Section 3 are reserved. You will need to locate the special reserve markers (or ropes) and place them properly prior to the service.

A periodic check needs to be made of the reserved pews to ensure they are ready for the special group. If you usher members of the special group to the pews or notice they are finding their own way, remove the markers and return them to their proper storage place.

A number of the items on the checklist sheet did not concern you. However, if your group uses a rotation system for service, you will be responsible for the various items on the sheet from time to time.

Doors Unlocked.—Never assume that another usher, the church custodian, or another church staff member has unlocked the doors. If you have the assignment, check the doors. Many a church member or visitor has waited outside the church building because of a locked door. A negative feeling can quickly be formed if it's raining outside and a person is trying to get through a locked door.

Temperature Control.—A church staff member may be the person responsible for setting the temperature control in your church building. If that's the case, you're lucky. In many churches the ushers have the duty.

You need to understand that no matter how well the temperature is controlled, someone will always be too hot or too cold.

Quickly changing temperatures outside affect the comfort temperature in the church building. Make sure you know the proper procedure to use for adjusting the inside temperature. Learn how to read the markings on the thermostat. The figures on some thermostats may be difficult to read properly, and you may miss the desired degree setting. Always double-check the degree setting listed on your checklist.

If your church is involved in a TV ministry, special attention needs to be given to temperature changes caused by the heat from required lighting.

Light Control.—Lights for the sanctuary may be controlled from the front or back of the room. You will need to be familiar with the specific location of the control switches in your church building. Be familiar also with the location and operation of the main circuit box. You may need to reset a breaker or replace a fuse in an emergency.

Newer church buildings may have dimmer switches. The pastor may desire that the lights be dimmed at various times. You need to be ready to comply in a skillful manner with a standard or spur-of-the-moment request.

Lighting for a night service will need your attention inside and outside the building. Lights for the parking area may or may not be on an automatic timer. Know how and from which switch they are controlled.

PA systems and steeple chimes are not on the checklist, but many smaller or older church buildings do have these items. Most often the controls for these items are located together. You should at least know how to turn these two pieces of equipment off. You may not be required to activate the equipment, but you do need to know how to control it in the event of a malfunction.

Each ushering group will have unique items to prepare and matters to handle. All of your serving area responsibilities have not been listed in this section; nor do they appear on the checklist. But you do recognize the necessity to check out your assigned area and be prepared to serve to the best of your ability.

Now that you, your fellow ushers, and the assigned service areas are properly prepared, it's time to greet the people.

Greeting the People

Some of the most intense yet most enjoyable times will come when you are greeting church members and visitors. You will need to be mentally awake and have your wits about you.

Greeting a member or visitor can take place in any area or at any time during your service. You will be called on to give your very best. Your warmth, your smile, your patience, your concern, your sociability— all come into play when you encounter another person.

Choose your words of greeting carefully. Some standard greetings are:

"Welcome, it's good to see you."

"Good morning. Welcome to our church."

"Hello, welcome to Fairview Church."

You can add variety to your greeting with a personal name and a question or comment.

"Mrs. Knight, good morning. How are you feeling today?"

"Good morning, Mrs. Knight. Isn't this a beautiful Lord's Day?"

"Hello, Mrs. Knight. I'm glad you're here today."

You will develop your own unique greeting style. The more you greet, the more comfortable and skilled you will become. Even with your own style, there are a few basic elements to greeting that you need to keep in mind.

Never Embarrass the Other Person.—The church members are your friends, and the visitors are the special guests of the church. You do not want to offend either.

Your attempts at a greeting can cause uneasiness and, at times, embarrassment if you are not careful. Note some simple greetings that begin fine but turn out sour.

> "Good morning, Mr. Knight. Where have you been hiding the last few months?"

> "Welcome, Mr. Knight. You sold any of those lemons on your car lot lately?"

> "Hello, Mr. Knight. Are you wearing another new suit?"

A basic principle for greeting is, greet others as you want to be greeted.

Shaking Hands.—A warm greeting and a firm handshake are tied together. Both actions unite to say welcome. The handshake is an expected part of your greeting. Men extend their right hands naturally in the tradition of trust and friendship. Most women feel the same freedom related to shaking hands.

In some cases, however, a person may not respond to your extended hand. No problem; you made the gesture. Don't take the lack of response personally.

There is probably a very good reason for the action.

Remember that a firm handshake is what is called for in greeting. Don't clamp down with a vicelike grip. And don't offer a dead fish handshake. Practice until you determine a feel for the proper firmness.

Never shake hands while wearing gloves. The personal touch is needed. If gloves are worn by your ushering group, it will be best for those in the greeting areas to go without gloves. Gloves add a nice touch to the ushers who are seating folk in the sanctuary.

A word about handshaking with an amputee. Extend your right hand as usual. The other person will respond appropriately. Don't switch hands; the amputee will handle the situation better than you. In like fashion, make no adjustment in your routine if the other person has an artificial hand. The other person will appreciate you for treating him in a normal fashion.

Guard Against Undue Familiarity.—Some people are huggers. It's their way of greeting friends. The same people may exchange kisses on the cheek. You may not be able to avoid a hugger. Don't be shocked or embarrassed if you're on the receiving end. However, do not initiate a hug unless you are completely certain that the other person is a willing receiver. Your reputation and usefulness as an usher will be greatly damaged if you are labeled as one who has roving hands.

Some people do not like to be touched by strangers. That's what you are to a visitor and some church

members. Some husbands are very protective of their
wives. Some mothers are very protective of their
children when touching is involved. Be aware of these
facts and don't overstep your bounds. Use your good
common sense.

Guard Against Favoritism.—You heard a phrase from
your parents, your teachers, and your friends when
you were a child—"Don't Play Favorites." The same
advice is good for you as an adult and a church
usher—"Don't Play Favorites." The temptation will be
available, but don't yield.

Treat each person you greet as a person of worth.
Take the time to be warm and caring with all you
encounter. The poorest member deserves the same
warm greeting you give to the richest member. Both
need to sense that they are people of worth. And
where better to have that feeling than at church?

The Epistle of James, in chapter 2:1-4, dealt with the
matter of favoritism in the early church. Note these
words:

> My brethren, do not hold your faith in our
> glorious Lord Jesus Christ with an attitude of
> personal favoritism.
>
> For if a man comes into your assembly
> with a gold ring and dressed in fine clothes,
> and there also comes in a poor man in dirty
> clothes,
>
> and you pay special attention to the one
> who is wearing the fine clothes, and say, "You
> sit here in a good place," and you say to the
> poor man, "You stand over there, or sit down
> by my footstool,"

have you not made distinctions among yourselves, and become judges with evil motives? (NASB)

As you have read, a lot is required of you before the worship service begins. The key is to be prepared. You can do it. Others are depending on you.

4
At Work During the Worship Service

You will recognize immediately that there is a measure of overlap related to the time you give to greeting, meeting, and seating. All three functions could take less than a minute with some church members or visitors. Other folk will require more attention and demand more of your time.

Somewhere between the two extremes is where you will want to concentrate your efforts. Take the time required to perform your function properly, but remember that other folk may be waiting to be greeted, met, and seated.

The size of your usher group may dictate that you perform the functions of greeting, meeting, and seating each time you serve. Or you may be assigned to just one function and rotate to the other functions on different Sundays. In either case, there are some factors you need to consider as you serve as meeter and seater. Your attention in this chapter also needs to be given to your fourth function, helping.

Meet the People

Somewhere between the time you greet a person and seat him is a segment of very valuable time. A

number of thoughtful deeds on your part can help put a visitor at ease or make a church member glad she came to church. You may routinely do some of the following. If not, hopefully you will discover some new helps for meeting people.

Guest Register.—Many churches like to have visitors sign the guest register in the vestibule. You are the obvious one to direct the visitor to the register, explaining its purpose. This also gives you time to inquire about the visitor's address and reason for visiting. In the question and answer exchange you may discover some information that allows you to move deeper into the conversation or gives you some clues to use as you introduce the visitor to other ushers and members. Here's a possible brief conversation between you and a visitor to illustrate the point.

> **You:** "Good morning. Welcome to our church. Is this your first visit with us?"
>
> **Visitor:** "Yes, it is."
>
> **You:** "I'm _____ . And your name is?"
>
> **Visitor:** "Charles Evans."
>
> **You:** "Charles, we would be pleased if you would sign our guest register. It's right over here."
>
> **Visitor:** "Thanks, I'll be happy to sign."
>
> **You:** "Oh, I notice you're from Tampa. We had a young couple unite with our church recently from Tampa. Their names are also Evans."

> **Visitor:** "Yes, that's my son and his wife. I'm to meet them here this morning for worship."
>
> **You:** "Charles, I'll walk into the sanctuary with you and help you locate your son and his wife. Here's a copy of today's bulletin."

If you had the time, you would want to introduce Charles Evans to other ushers nearby or members who might be in the vestibule.

Introductions.—Although most people consider introductions a normal everyday activity, few take the time to master the proper procedure for this important event.

New freedoms in our society have brought some changes to the proper etiquette of introductions. However, there are still a few standard rules involved. If a younger and older person are the subjects to be introduced, the younger is always introduced to the older.

> "Mrs. Smith, I want you to know Sally. She'll be in our Youth Department."
>
> "Sally, I want to introduce you to Mrs. Smith."

When you are introducing a male and female and you judge their ages to be approximately the same, the female's name is mentioned first.

> "Ann, may I introduce Stan."
>
> "Ann Wright, Stan Cole."

You may usher in a church where a number of the members and frequent visitors hold high positions in the military, are elected officials, or have made noted achievements in life that sets them apart. In this case, you introduce the less important to the more important.

"Dr. Joan Sharp, may I introduce Ed Turner."

"Ed Turner, I want to introduce you to Mayor Cook."

"General Williams, may I present our pastor's wife, Mrs. Cole."

Don't overdo your introductions. But be careful that you don't underdo them either. When you are in doubt about age, rank, or importance of a person, do the best you can with your introductions. The important thing is to help people become acquainted.

Special Help.—The meeting time with visitors allows you time to be observant and helpful. This is also a time for sharing items related to your church programs. As time allows, share appropriate information.

- the baby care program
- the Bible study program
- training opportunities
- music program
- the historical room
- other worship services

A visitor may request directions for travel to use after the worship service. She may want to know about restaurants, motels, or recreation facilities. You should be prepared to share clear and correct information or call in another usher to help. Some churches have a list of these facilities printed and share it when a request is made. Know where these lists are and make them available.

Always look and listen for clues from visitors that will allow you to be of maximum help and service.

Today's Worship Service.—If you have taken the time to study the bulletin for the worship service, you may want to point out any special features as you share a bulletin with a visitor or member. You may comment that the pastor is beginning a series of sermons this morning on a special theme. You may want to point out that today's soloist is a noted musician.

If your church is broadcasting live, the visitor may be interested in knowing the call letters of the station. If the broadcast is delayed, point this out to the visitor.

A personal word about the service will be another opportunity to make the visitor and member feel a part of the worship experience.

Seating the People

All of your responsibilities are important. A warm greeting is basic. Time spent in meeting is essential. Seating is vital. In fact, many experienced ushers consider seating to be at the very center of their responsibilities.

Seating of visitors and members is so substantial that you and your fellow ushers need to constantly work at developing and upgrading your skills in this area. Proper seating requires more than directing a person to an empty pew. Let's examine the many facets of effective seating.

Study the Sanctuary.—You need to make a periodic check of the sanctuary to determine where the empty seats are. If the sanctuary has more than one entrance, seats can be filled rather quickly by the members without your help. You will know from experience where many members sit each service. You may know that certain members will be absent for a given service. This information will help as you seek to locate empty seats.

Your study of the sanctuary should help you determine any sound or temperature concerns. The sound system in your church building may create a hearing problem for some members. The problem may or may not be able to be corrected. In either event, you need to be aware of the problem should a person request a seat away from loud sounds.

The temperature may be uneven in the sanctuary. Open doors or windows could create a draft which members and visitors may need to avoid for health reasons. For various reasons, the congregation may need to live with the temperature problems. However, your knowledge of the sanctuary allows you to seat visitors and members according to their preferences.

Seating Preferences.—Many ushers suggest that seating preferences create problems for them at times. If the worship hour has not arrived and you are seating people, it's a good idea to ask whether they have a seating preference. However, when the service is under way, it's not wise to ask for a seating preference. You may or may not be able to fill the preference desire of a latecomer.

If a person indicates he will be leaving the service early, seat him on the aisle near the back of the sanctuary or near an exit door.

If a visitor indicates she has a hearing problem and needs a seat up front, you need to comply. Your church may be equipped with a sound system that allows for special hearing devices attached to the pews at the front of the sanctuary. When a guest is seated in this area, remain long enough to help the guest locate and adjust the hearing device.

You never know what personal preferences a guest may have about seating. You will need, however, to be ready to meet a specific request if at all possible. An usher was confronted with the following seating preference: A blind man and his Seeing Eye dog came to the worship service. The blind visitor requested a seat where his dog would not detract from the service.

Fortunately, the request came before the worship service began. The usher was able to seat the blind guest near the front. His dog remained under the pew next to his master. Not until the service was over did the majority of the congregation realize that the dog was in the service.

Seating Balance.—Knowing that most members take a seat in the same general area each service will be an aid to you as you try to keep seating balance in the sanctuary. You can help fill in the open spaces by seating or suggesting that folk be seated in these areas.

Your efforts at seating balance will be of special help to the pastor and the music leader. In fact, they can point out these open spaces if you get their input.

A general principle for seating balance is, seat forward when possible.

It's important also to seat visitors next to or near members. This procedure allows you to achieve balance and makes the visitors feel a part of the congregation. They are not isolated to a "visitors' section" in the sanctuary.

With your awareness of the seating needs of people in mind, let's turn attention to some mechanics of seating.

How to Seat.—You have probably been seated by an usher on different occasions. Did you notice the technique used by the usher? If you didn't notice anything special, the usher performed his duty well. The usher's actions were natural, and he moved with ease through the seating procedure. That's exactly how you should be. Your seating style needs to be natural and unhurried.

- Seating elderly people. This person can be male or female. Offer your right arm. You may hear "I'm fine" or "I can make it." That's a no-thank-you response to your offer. You are then free to move ahead. Walk slowly to the seat you are suggesting. Place your hand on the pew in front of the one you have selected and face your guest. This movement leaves no doubt to the guest which pew you have in mind.

  If the person has taken your arm, again walk slowly and suggest how far you are going. "Mrs. Wilson, I have a fine seat for you at the front."

  If a seating preference is requested, try your best to respond.

- Seating most people. When seating to your left, and the person has your arm, stop at the back of the pew you are suggesting. Gently guide your guest into the pew. If you are seating to your right, lower your right arm as an indication that you have reached the suggested seat. In either direction, right or left, you may need to assist the guest.

  This seating procedure will work if you are seating one person or a large family. Your main concern will be selecting the proper location to seat your guest.

- Seating those who slip by. Your human tendency will be to think, *if she wanted my help, she could have waited a few seconds.* But, being the positive usher you are, you will move down the aisle quickly to offer your assistance. No mention will be made to the person about the need for waiting. You simply assist the person in locating a seat.

No matter how near or how far an empty seat may be, never point to a seat as a substitute for ushering. Your responsibility is to seat, not point.

When to Seat.—This part of the seating procedure will need to be discussed with your pastor. He will need to suggest appropriate times during the worship service for visitors and members to be seated. This is, of course, after the stated time for the beginning of the service.

A sample order of worship from the bulletin of Fairview Church is printed on page 81. The features of the order of worship are clear and easy to read.

They are rather standard for many churches. Note, however, the last line of the bulletin, "*Those waiting will be seated by the ushers at this time." An asterisk (*) appears on various items to the left side of the bulletin. These notations are clear signs for you to use.

If there is a door between the vestibule and the sanctuary, you should see that it is closed when the worship service begins. Those who come late can be detained in the vestibule until an appropriate time for them to be ushered to a seat.

Look again at the sample order of worship. Note the five suggested opportunities for seating the latecomers. You may determine the need for more or fewer opportunities in your local church. Study the matter, work with your pastor, agree on the special seating times, and indicate the times on your church bulletin.

The special indications on the bulletin will aid you when it's necessary to detain latecomers in the vestibule. They will better understand the delay when you hand them a bulletin and share with them the next seating time.

Again, seating is vital. You can become a skilled seater with practice.

Help the People

Up to this point in your work as an usher you have been rather busy. You have made early preparation, greeted, met, and seated visitors and members. The worship service is under way. Time to relax? Well, not really. Now you may be called on to help with a few

FAIRVIEW CHURCH

*Prelude . . . . "Benedictus" . . . . Rowley

*Church Ministry Highlights

*Words Of Welcome

Invocation . . . . The Pastor

Call To Worship . . . . "Sound The Trumpet" . . . . Purcell
The Sanctuary Choir

*Hymn 40 . . . . "All Hail The Power Of . . . . *Coronation*
Jesus' Name"

Scripture

Pastoral Prayer

Quartet . . . . . "Praise The Lord, The King . . . . . arr. Reynolds
Of Glory"
Men's Quartet

*Hymn 208 . . . . "Like A River Glorious" . . . . *Wye Valley*

Giving Our Tithes And Offerings

Offertory . . . . "Abide, O Dearest Jesus" . . . . Peeters

Hymn 72 . . . . "Jesus, Thou Joy of . . . . *Quebec*
Loving Hearts"

Sermon . . . . "Learning To Pray" . . . . The Pastor

Hymn Of Commitment

Benediction

Postlude . . . . "Trumpet Tune" . . . . Stanley

*Those waiting will be seated by the ushers at this time.

other events. These come under the general heading of helping the people—pastor and congregation.

Helping the Pastor.—Most of what you do for the pastor during the service will be planned. If you are given the responsibility of helping distribute visitors' cards or packets, be ready when the pastor is ready. Many pastors will use cue phrases to help you. He may say, "As the ushers come . . . " or "The ushers have a card . . . " or "The ushers want to give you . . . . " Whatever the prearranged signal is, be ready.

You may have a planned part of helping to take the offering. The head usher will usually direct this activity for the pastor by indicating the part of the sanctuary you are to cover. Be sure you have your assignment clearly in mind. On a number of occasions ushers have been known to head for the choir loft, only to discover their fellow ushers headed in the same direction. Be certain you are clear in your instructions for the disposition of the offering.

The question is nearly always raised in usher training sessions, "What should I do if I drop the offering plate?" There are three things you need to do: (1) pick up the plate and as much of the offering as you can recover quickly, (2) face the embarrassment of the moment, and (3) learn from the experience.

Dropping the plate can happen to you whether you are ushering for the first time, have years of ushering experience, usher in a large church, or usher in a small church.

Some pastors request the ushers to count the congregation. If this is an activity you are involved in, know the procedure used to secure a correct count.

Provide the information in the form the pastor has requested. This could be a verbal message or a written note.

Probably the most unplanned thing you will do to help the pastor is take him notes to the pulpit. Hopefully, your pastor has shared in a training session for you what he considers essential and nonessential information to be shared with him during the worship service.

The head usher usually handles the note-sharing activity for your group. However, you may be assigned the responsibility by the head usher.

You will need to determine and judge what is essential information to share with the pastor (if he has not made his wishes known). You will need to consider what the pastor is doing before you take action. A general rule may help: share essential information up to the time of the sermon; interrupt the sermon only when the information is life threatening.

Helping the Congregation.—The best thing you can do to help the congregation is to do your job and see that activities and actions are performed smoothly. Anytime your actions call attention to you during the worship service, a part of the congregation has diverted their attention to you.

At the appropriate time, usually just prior to the sermon, you and your fellow ushers will go to assigned places for the remainder of the worship service. You will continue to have specific yet varied responsibilities.

• Outside the Building. You may be assigned to

monitor the parking lot. You may be able to perform this task from inside the building by watching from a window, or you may need to be physically present on the lot. The security you provide frees the congregation of one less worry during their worship experience. You will also be able to assist, as needed, latecomers and early leavers.

- Other Parts of the Building. Some congregations require their ushers to provide building security during a worship service. This request may be for both inside and outside the building. If this is true in your case, determine exactly what is to be done.

- In the Vestibule. At least two of your group need to be assigned to provide assistance in the vestibule. Your responsibilities will vary in this area of the building during the worship service. You will have latecomers who need to be seated. People may leave the service early and need your assistance.

The church's telephone system may have an extension in the vestibule and all incoming calls are received there during the worship service.

Many ushers of downtown churches are required to deal with those people who walk off the street seeking some type of help. If these folk have come to worship, by all means greet and seat them as you would any visitor. If their need is otherwise, use the church's standard procedure or your best judgment for handling the situation.

- In the Sanctuary. While you are seated in the sanctuary, you are still functioning as an usher. You are ready to aid the pastor should he make a request. You are prepared to move quickly to handle emergencies.

  Study Floor Plan 2 on page 86. You are assigned to section 1 of the sanctuary and positioned to survey your section. You are assigned to position C. The arrows indicate the directions you should have under surveillance.

  You should have a general knowledge of the members in your assigned section. Should the need arise, you could call for the help of a doctor, nurse, policeman, fireman, or others to help.

As with any list of responsibilities, you will need to translate the matters mentioned in this chapter into your own local church situation.

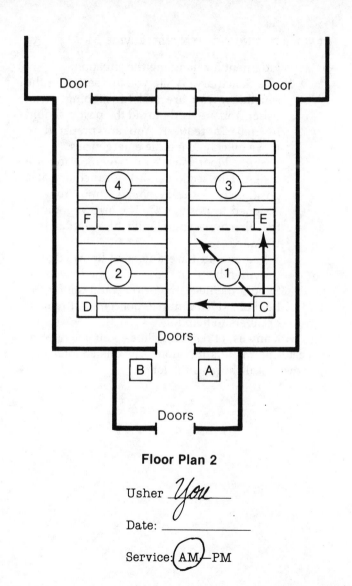

Floor Plan 2

Usher *You*

Date: _____

Service: AM—PM

5
At Work After the Worship Service

Soon after the final word is spoken by your pastor or the final note is sounded by the choir, the great exodus begins. Church members and visitors alike head for the exits. Your temptation will be to get in the flow and move along with the others.

If you're an off-duty usher, your movement out of the sanctuary will encourage others to do the same. However, if you are an on-duty usher, a few things are yet to be cared for before you leave the church building.

Let's examine your responsibilities after the worship service in three areas: (1) the people, (2) the building, and (3) the reports.

The People

An usher commented, "I'm glad we don't usher people out of the sanctuary. If we did, we'd have a lot of mad people." Have you noticed it takes a lot less time to empty the sanctuary than it does to fill it? People are moving on to their other opportunities and adventures of the day.

Even with the hurried movement, you can still find

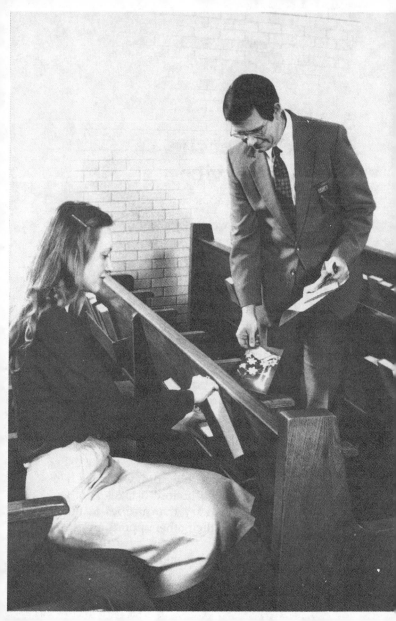

opportunities to meet and help people. There is not a set priority for your functions after the service, but common sense will dictate your actions.

Helping the Elderly.—If you helped seat an elderly person at the beginning of the service, you should check to determine whether the same person needs help now. If you do help, look around the pew for any items the elderly person may leave behind. Sometimes Bibles get dropped under the pew or stuck in the hymnal rack. Articles of clothing also have a way of falling under the pew.

Quite often you will discover that someone else is helping the elderly person. That's fine and allows you to move to other individuals and responsibilities. But do remember to check.

Greeting and Meeting the Visitors.—You may have time for only a brief greeting with visitors who are on their way out of the sanctuary. Visitors' tags or ribbons will quickly identify them to you. If you greeted them at the beginning of the worship service, remember to call them by name if possible.

Unhurried visitors will allow you more time to meet them after the service. Don't try and monopolize all their time. Introduce them to others around. If, of course, the visitor should request help and you can give it, take the time required.

Many pastors like to offer a special greeting to visitors after the worship service. You can help visitors by directing them to the pastor and make the proper introductions.

If you have been seated in the sanctuary during the sermon, you will spot the visitors in your section.

Make a special effort to greet these guests. If you have been seated in the vestibule during the service, most of the visitors will pass by you as they leave. You may not be able to shake hands with all who pass, but you can say a word of greeting and a friendly "come back and visit with us again."

Greeting and Meeting the Members.—You may see the same members each Sunday, but it's still important to greet and meet them. Nurture your long-standing friendship with your fellow church members. A wave of your hand or a smile from a distance will show your acknowledgment of them if you are not able to have a personal conversation.

Many church buildings lend themselves to the members sharing with each other before and after the worship service. The vestibule, large or small, is a natural meeting place for you and the members. When all of your other duties are completed, take time to circulate in the vestibule, greeting and meeting your church friends.

Handling Emergencies.—You have been reminded of your responsibility for emergencies during the first two phases of the worship service, before and during. You also must be ready to handle emergencies after the service. Keep your eyes and ears open for sights and sounds that indicate an emergency is at hand.

Emergencies are covered in the next chapter. But for now, be aware and be ready after the service.

The Building

Your greeting and meeting people after the service must be done in relationship to your responsibility to care for the church building. You should be able to do both activities simultaneously. You may be headed for a visitor several pews away while collecting discarded bulletins. You could be talking with a church friend while closing a door or window.

There are two parts of the church building that will demand your attention after the service, the sanctuary and the vestibule.

The Sanctuary.—You probably will know ahead of time what to look for in the sanctuary after the service. If you have not been instructed, begin in the choir loft and work your way to the rear of the sanctuary. Check the aisles, the pews, the floor area under the pews, the pulpit area, and the windowsills.

Some ushering groups use a checklist to ensure that all areas are covered. Generally, you will find items like the following:

- Discarded bulletins and other paper
- Articles of clothing
- Bibles, books, and hymnals
- Magazines and leaflets
- Purses and billfolds
- Keys, eyeglasses, and umbrellas

Your final trip through the sanctuary will give you the opportunity to check on doors that adjoin the sanctuary, windows, sound system, lights, and other equipment that may need to be turned off.

Basically, you are getting the sanctuary ready for the next service. You will need to know where trash is to be taken so you can deposit the throwaway items. Take the other items to the lost-and-found box or room. Note any item with an identification marking.

You will read a little later in the chapter why this is important.

The Vestibule.—Again, like the sanctuary, you are preparing the vestibule for the next service. Chances are that you are also preparing the vestibule for another team of ushers. You will want to leave everything in good order for your fellow ushers. The better you prepare the vestibule, the more time the next group of ushers will have to use in greeting and meeting.

Throw away unneeded items. Take items left in the sanctuary and vestibule to the lost and found. You may have noticed that some items keep reappearing in the same areas.

Probably one of your fellow ushers had good intentions about removing the items but failed to follow through. In some cases the vestibule may be your church's lost and found. If that's true, place the items in some order rather than throwing them in a dark corner.

Return the offering plates to their proper place if they are kept in the vestibule. Do the same for any items that will be used by the next ushering team. Your fellow ushers need to depend on you to store such items as identification badges and ribbons, usher flowers, pew markers (reserved), visitors' cards or packets, and so forth.

Take a quick look around the vestibule. Remove any posters advertising an event that was completed with the service just concluded. Do the same with any seasonal display that will be dated the next time the vestibule is used. There is probably a proper storage place for seasonal decorations used in the vestibule. A note to the head usher or a call to the church office will be your reminder to them to handle the dated items.

Place the temperature control on the proper setting. Close and lock any outside windows. Turn out the lights. Close and lock the doors. If your door is double, the type with the top and bottom latch, make certain the latches are secure. Your careful lockup procedure may prevent a break-in. Be as careful with your church as you are with the security of your own home.

At some point before you leave the church building or shortly after you arrive home, two reports should be completed.

The Reports

When the subject is mentioned, you may think as a lot of ushers do, "I never knew ushers had to fill out reports." Well, it's not really as bad as you might think. You probably are already doing a form of reporting. You may be sharing with the head usher the usual and unusual events of the service. You may feel that verbal reporting is sufficient, but a growing number of churches are asking for a written report from the head usher related to each worship service. You will be feeding information to the head usher that helps make up the official report. Or, in the absence of the head usher, you may be the one completing the report. Let's examine the first of the two reports needed.

For the Church.—You may better appreciate the

importance of a report to the church when you learn
the purposes for the report. Here are some purposes
churches have shared:

- to compile a complete and accurate history of
  the church
- to have an accurate record of unusual events
- to help the members recover lost items
- to have a record of emergencies and how they
  were handled
- to have a record of the ushers serving
- to provide input for the building and grounds
  committee
- to share information with the pastor and staff
- to have a record of worship attendance

As you recognize, a lot of needed and helpful
information can be shared. You will have firsthand
facts about the service you usher that must be shared.

The sample Usher Report (p. 97) is one similar to
that used by many churches. The information requested is rather standard, and it becomes vital to the
record system of your church. As with any form, you
will need to translate the sample given into the
information needs of your local church situation.

You need to have an illustration of an actual happening which validates the importance of and need
for an usher report. Usher Lee served a church that
had a balcony around three sides of the sanctuary.
After the worship service one Sunday morning, he
was making a routine check. He walked down the
center aisle, over to the outside aisle, and started to
the back of the church.

Then he noticed a light-colored powder next to the

wall. He examined the substance and found it to be gritty in nature. Usher Lee shared his discovery with the head usher and a note was made on the report, "Checked the aisle under the balcony on the right side—cleanup needed."

The cleanup request was shared with the custodian, who, upon inspection, found not a little gritty powder but a large amount. The custodian's report to the pastor prompted a thorough inspection of the area. The balcony was pulling away from the outside wall due to a weak support structure. The gritty powder was the first outward sign of an unsafe balcony.

The usher who discovered the problem and reported it may have prevented a terrible accident in the church building. A verbal remark could have been enough to uncover the problem. But a written report found its way to the proper desk and alerted others to investigate.

For Yourself.—The second type of report is for you. This report doesn't necessarily need to be written, but some ushers do find it helpful to record events and look back on them at later times.

You can create your own format for reporting. Some ushers have enjoyed recording their experiences in a diary or journal. Others keep a file folder at their home and drop notes in the folder about their experiences. You may be one of the brave ones and trust your memory to recall the events you have experienced.

In addition to recording experiences and events of your career as an usher, you may want to note people you meet, thoughts you have for improvement, ideas you want to share and try, or other information you may want to remember in the future. Regardless of the method you choose for remembering your experiences, make use of the information to evaluate yourself.

Think through the events you were involved in. Recall positive and negative feelings you had. Ask yourself questions such as, *Did I make proper preparation for my service? Did I seek to be helpful today?* Tally those and other thoughts you have about your effort and then ask, *How have I grown as an usher?* If you have not identified any growth, you have some work to do.

Routine may be the best word to describe your responsibilities after the close of the worship service. Work to create a routine that is thorough in coverage and gives you a peace of mind that all matters have been handled properly.

Usher Report

_____ AM   PM
(date)

Ushers Serving:

Number in the Congregation:

Emergencies:

Repairs Needed:

Noteworthy Lost Items:

Information for the Pastor/Staff:

Signed: _____

6
Dealing with the Unexpected

Unless you are skilled at using a crystal ball to look into the future, you will be forced, like other ushers, to deal with unexpected events as they happen. There are many things you will do routinely each time you usher. You will develop your own unique style, and many activities will be done naturally. You will perform many of your responsibilities without much thought. All of this is good and as it should be.

However, how you handle the unexpected—the emergencies—will not be totally routine, natural, or thoughtless. You must be ready when the emergency occurs. You may be helping other ushers handle an emergency, or you may be the only usher available. The proper handling of an emergency may be your responsibility totally.

There are some general thoughts you can commit to memory; you can practice handling emergencies; and you can talk with other ushers about handling emergencies. Consider two areas of general thoughts related to handling emergencies: things to do and things to know.

Things to Do

When you encounter an emergency, a number of things will enter your mind. Your random thoughts may include a series of questions: What's the problem? Who or what is involved? What action is required?

These split-second questions often require split-second answers. Some of your thinking and resulting actions will come from instinct. Other actions will result after you have given the situation a little more thought. In some cases, only a few seconds will pass between the instinct and thinking stages.

For example, you are ushering an elderly person to a pew. Halfway down the aisle the person stops and begins to fall. Instinctively, you try to break his fall.

Probably before the person reaches the floor you have already thought, *What's the problem? What needs to be done?* You recognize that the time between instinct and thinking is brief. In other cases the thinking time is longer.

In any emergency there are at least five things you can do.

Be Prepared to Act.—You must keep your basic senses sharp at all times when you usher. Your sight, hearing, and sense of smell must be ever alert to the activity around you. You will become, if you are not already, accustomed to the usual sights, sounds, and smells of the normal day at church. But the unusual sights, sounds, and smells will warn you of a pending emergency or one in progress.

You need to develop the skill of distinguishing

between the usual and the unusual. The piercing yell of a child coming down a hallway to the vestibule may be usual, but the same piercing yell from an adult is unusual and a sign that your attention is needed.

The smell of a candle burning may be usual in your church, but the smell of wood or rubber burning is entirely different. You must be prepared to act when the unusual presents itself.

No matter what you are doing at the time, an emergency must take priority. If you are greeting a visitor and the unusual catches your attention, politely and calmly excuse yourself.

However, if you notice that the emergency is being cared for by your fellow ushers, continue with your responsibilities. You will not only need to be aware of your assigned area but also be conscious of the unattended area.

Your preparation to act must be coupled with your quick action.

Be Quick in Action.—The time it takes you to act in an emergency may be the difference between success and failure, triumph and defeat, life and death.

You may be the only usher available to respond to an emergency. Your actions will be vital to solving the unexpected situation. You must think and act quickly. Call for the help of another usher if needed. Or enlist the help of another person nearby.

If you come upon an emergency and you know help is on the way, size up the situation and be ready to take charge. Direct the handling of the emergency. Give orders until a more knowledgeable person arrives. Each emergency requires someone to take charge to bring the situation under control. Do not hesitate to act, but do not hesitate.

Be Calm.—All emergencies require quick action and demand calmness. The usher who smells smoke and runs down the center aisle yelling "Fire! Fire!" has probably created a greater emergency by his erratic action than the smoke itself.

You will not find it easy to remain calm in most situations. When life-threatening emergencies occur you will have the tendency to tense up, to overreact, to panic, to act erratically, or to express other unusual behavior.

A wise usher suggested he had to practice being calm. He would try to mentally simulate emergencies and then place himself in the scene. He tried to feel the experience and his role in handling the emergency. He would then evaluate himself and his actions.

This is one method to use to practice being calm. Some ushers have shared that a deep breath helped them to stay calm and in control while handling an emergency.

Whatever method you devise, staying calm is so important for facing and solving emergencies. Your personal calmness may be the one critical factor that prevents an unexpected situation from getting out of control.

Be Thorough in Direction.—Many emergencies will require your quick action. All will demand your calmness. Some situations will develop and get out of hand if thorough directions are not given. Too many small situations have turned into major emergencies because an usher gave general rather than specific instructions.

Examine the following: Mrs. Glass comes to the front door of the church and says to Usher Nelson, "I'm having a problem with my car. I think I smelled smoke. Could you check it?" Usher Nelson lifts the hood, starts the car, and sure enough the smoke begins to billow.

Usher Nelson senses a fire. "Mrs. Glass," directs Usher Nelson, "Please hurry and ask one of the other ushers to come out and help me." Note the general directions.

In a few seconds a second usher arrives, only to see a burning car. If Usher Nelson had been thorough in his directions, he could probably have prevented a major emergency.

When Usher Nelson shared his experience with his fellow ushers, his self-evaluation was a learning time for all. Usher Nelson commented, "I could have saved Mrs. Glass's car if only I had told her one more thing. 'Please hurry and ask one of the other ushers to bring me a fire extinguisher.'"

Be thorough in giving directions. You may have only one chance.

Be Directive.—Most ushers you serve with and those you meet in other situations are nondirective. They, like you, are very easygoing and seek to keep things in harmony.

When you are handling emergencies you may need to step out of character and be very directive. You will need to have this understanding with your fellow ushers, and you will need to recognize this characteristic in them. Someone needs to give orders and be directive. Someone needs to take charge when an emergency occurs.

If a church member has fallen and a crowd is gathering around to look, you may need to say, "Please move along and keep this area clear." Your tone of voice may not be pleasing to some, but in this case you're not trying to be pleasing.

Each emergency will be different. Yet each will be demanding. Remember that there are some things you can do.

Things to Know

Listed below are the results of a brainstorming and discussion activity conducted with a group of ushers, like you, in a training session. The question asked was: What are some things you need to know to properly handle an emergency? After the activity the ideas generated were discussed and placed in categories. The categories are probably ones you would likewise identify—What? Where? Who?

The "What" Things to Know.—What is an emergency? You will be called on to judge many situations to determine whether an emergency exists. You don't have a list that determines an answer for you. So your judgment is the key. You will be able to judge some situations as emergencies and be correct every time. Other situations will occur, your judgment will indicate that no emergency exists, and you will be wrong.

Look at two examples: First, on a very warm Sunday as the congregation is leaving the sanctuary, a lady faints in the vestibule. Second, on the same

Sunday a small child tugs on your hand and states, "I can't find my mommy." The child begins to cry.

Are both situations emergencies? Some ushers have said yes to the question. Other ushers have said no. In both illustrations you must make a judgment. By the way, most ushers identified the two illustrations as emergencies but with different intensity.

What items are available to help handle the emergency? The generated list included:

- telephone and a listing of emergency numbers
- list and location of the area hospitals
- fire extinguishers
- first-aid kit
- wheelchair

The "Where" Things to Know.—This list will help you remember certain items whose locations you should know in order to help handle an emergency.

- location of the telephone
- location of fire extinguishers
- location of exits
- location of first-aid kit
- location of wheelchair
- location in the sanctuary of professional people who have knowledge to handle an emergency

The "Who" Things to Know.—The professions listed represent people who could be available to any congregation. However, the size of your church congregation may add to or delete from the list.

- medical doctor
- nurse
- policeman

- fire fighter
- auto mechanic
- building contractor
- plumber
- electrician
- heating/cooling mechanic
- sound engineer
- individuals with CPR training

The things you know about handling emergencies will need to be updated as changes occur with the what, where, and who information available.

Practice Handling Emergencies

You may think it strange to suggest that you practice handling emergencies. But practice will give you a feel for the actual emergency situation. You will be able to think through your participation in the situation, note the way you brought the situation under control, and recognize what you learned from your own self-evaluation. Then, hopefully, when you are faced with a real emergency, similar to the ones practiced, you can respond in a helpful manner.

Seven emergency situations are described in the paragraphs that follow. These situations are typical of ones mentioned and experienced by other ushers. Place yourself in charge of handling the situations.

Musical Fallout.—The worship service at your church is under way on a hot and humid July Sunday morning. The sanctuary is a little warm, but the choir loft is reaching the uncomfortable stage. Halfway through the choir special, Mr. Wilkins in the bass section falls to his chair and slumps over. You have observed the entire scene. You are the usher nearest the choir loft. Respond.

Dog Gone.—The congregation is standing and singing a hymn. You are seating a latecomer. You turn to return to the vestibule, and coming down the aisle is a dog. As you approach the dog, he begins to bark and darts under an empty pew. Respond.

Hear Me.—Your pastor is preaching the morning sermon. You are seated on the back pew. You notice a lady stand, move out of her pew to the middle aisle, face the pastor, and begin to yell at him. Respond.

What Will I Do?—You are standing in the vestibule, and an elderly lady approaches you. She is visibly nervous. She says, "I've lost my purse. My checkbook, credit cards, and money are in my purse. They're all gone. What will I do?" Respond.

Pew Sickness.—A man, with his five-year-old son in his arms, comes to the vestibule from the sanctuary. The sour smell suggests that someone is sick. The father turns to you and exclaims, "I'm afraid my son created a mess in there. He threw up before I could get him out. You may need to check with some of the people who were near us. Sorry." Respond.

Where There's Smoke.—Your church has a rather large vestibule. You have closed the doors between the vestibule and sanctuary because the worship service has begun. You smell smoke and discover that one of the bathrooms in the corner of the vestibule is ablaze. Respond.

Down and Out.—It's a cold winter Sunday. The wind is blowing in strong gusts. The front door is closed to keep out as much cold air as possible. Usher

Taylor is standing near the front door looking out the diamond-shaped window. This allows him to open the door as someone approaches. Usher Taylor is talking to you with his back to the door. The door opens, striking Usher Taylor in the head, and he falls to the floor unconscious. Respond.

Remember, the way you practice is the way you will perform when a real emergency occurs.

Talk with Other Ushers

You could interview any number of ushers who serve churches through the land and discover some very unusual emergencies. The more ushers you can ask about how they handle emergencies, the better prepared you will be to handle unexpected situations in your church.

You will talk to a number of persons each week who attend churches other than yours. These are people you know in your community, work with, or serve with in various organizations. Some of these individuals serve their own churches as ushers. Swapping information related to ushering can be good and helpful for both of you.

When you travel on vacation and attend other churches, be aware of the ushers. Note things they do in handling emergencies. If time is available, talk with the ushers after the worship service.

Of course, you should find the time to talk with the other ushers in your own church. Some ushering groups are large enough to be divided into teams. You should know how emergencies are handled by your usher team.

You may need to make an extra effort to discover the activities of the other ushering teams.

Talking and sharing with other ushers will allow all of you to grow and be better prepared to respond to this important part of your responsibilities.

7
Ushers for All Seasons

Your key phrase in this brief chapter is all seasons. Your church will observe special events and be involved in special emphases during the year. You probably will be called on to usher for many of these special happenings.

In some cases you may be called on to provide training and leadership for a special emphasis during which the regular ushers are not assigned. You also may be called on to help usher at some very happy and very sad occasions. So all seasons extend your ushering opportunities beyond your regular duties.

When you usher for special events, emphases, or different occasions, your roles and functions may vary slightly. You may be required to do things a little differently and place more emphasis in some areas than in others. So that you will be ready for all seasons, consider some of the following details.

Special Events

As always, your church will be unique in many of the special events it promotes. You can add the special events of your church to the following events suggested by other ushers.

Revivals.—A usual characteristic of revival meetings is informality. Your basic ushering functions for the revival will be the same as in a regular worship service. However, the air of informality could affect greeting, meeting, and seating activities.

Your guest evangelist may want the church members in the congregation to make a special effort to welcome the visitors. The music leader may request special things of the congregation. These special activities are usually unplanned and will require you to adjust your seating procedure at times.

You may be called on to reserve pews for special groups during the revival. Your special attention will need to be given to this matter as you seat folk.

Standard events of a regular worship service such as recognition of guests, the offering, and special music may change during the revival services. The pastor may or may not share special instructions with you. So you will need to pay close attention to the activities in the sanctuary.

Homecomings.—Like revival services, homecomings are special events that will demand your special attention and extra effort. All of your functions will be intensified. You will be greeting folk from out of town who are former members, some of whom you may not know. You may tend to meet with old friends and/or former members longer than usual. This could crowd the vestibule at times. Seating could present problems as old friends request seats together.

Special attention may be given to the guests in the

worship service. The pastor may change his usual procedure of guest recognition. Be prepared to comply with his wishes should you be involved in the activity.

You will need to be ready to handle emergencies created by the events of the day such as parking, extra chairs for the sanctuary, directional information, and so forth.

Church Group Meetings.—Your church building may be the meeting place for multichurch gatherings. Your usher group and other usher groups may be combined for these large meetings. If this is the case, it would be wise for your group and the other ushers to meet together.

You can walk through the building pointing out the features all ushers need to know. The same approach should be used if you are asked to participate as an usher at another church. You will need a general knowledge of the facilities.

Such meetings with mixed ushering groups will require that all ushers be prepared to give and take and work as a unified team.

Holidays.—Your church may conduct special worship services centered around holidays. The special holiday events may add extra responsibilities for you. Holiday services may bring extra visitors to your worship services. Be prepared to handle all the activities your church plans for and with visitors during these special services.

The routine you follow during a regular worship service may need to be altered for special holiday services. Check the bulletin as usual and be prepared.

Special Emphases

Your participation in special emphases will probably involve you in training other ushers. Consider two special emphases—youth and women. The guidance you give these two groups can be applied to other groups as well.

Youth Emphasis.—Your church may set aside a week each year for the youth to share the major responsibilities of church leadership. Your involvement with the youth can be a happy one if you will remember that they are youth and not adults.

If you are called on to help the youth ushers, give them the basics of greeting, meeting, and seating. You will want to retain the responsibility for handling all emergencies. In fact, you may need to stay in the vestibule while the youth are serving. You can give your support as they go about their duties.

Remember this about youth: They are the church leaders of tomorrow. Do a good job of training them for their special opportunity because you may also be training ushers for the future.

Women's Emphasis.—These emphases are rather standard in many churches and probably are in yours. Your role will be similar to that for helping youth—sharing the basics of greeting, meeting, and seating. Be available to support the special effort and to handle the emergencies.

One head usher shared the following: "One time a year we have an all-male choir. During that service the ladies take total charge of the ushering responsibilities." Another usher said that during any special women's emphasis the regular female ushers take the full responsibility for enlisting and training other ladies to help.

Special emphases are special times in your church and call for special help from you. Be prepared to be special with your help and support.

Happy and Sad Occasions

All seasons include happy and sad occasions. The most representative happy occasion is a wedding. The most representative sad occasion is a funeral. You may be asked to usher at both. There are some special features to both occasions that need your attention.

Happy Occasions.—Ushering for a wedding is a fun experience. You will be able to use your ushering skills to help your friends on this very special and happy occasion.

Probably the bride will have a wedding consultant to help her with the details of the wedding. Or the bride may ask you to handle all the ushering respon-sibilities. If the latter is true, be sure to coordinate your responsibilities in relationship to times in the ceremony and individuals involved. You will need answers to the following concerns:

- when to light candles (if used)
- what the special seating requests or instruc-tions are
- when to seat the mothers and other family members
- who will seat and usher out the mothers
- when to pull the aisle runner (if used)
- what role the ushers will play at the reception

Basically, your greeting will be limited to a smile

and a brief word of welcome. Remember, no handshaking if you are wearing gloves. Position yourself to the left in the vestibule. You will be offering your right arm to the ladies you usher and seat.

If you have been instructed to offer a seating preference, ask the guest: Friend of the bride? Friend of the groom? Seat the guest accordingly. If no special instructions are given, seat for balance. You will want to review the content in this book related to seating.

If the individuals helping you usher are new to the experience, take the time to share the basic procedure involved in seating. Give as much help and instruction as you can in the time you have available.

Your part in the wedding is a gift you give to the bride and groom. Give them the gift you would want to receive.

Sad Occasions.—Your final tribute to a friend may come in a sad way. You may be requested to usher the funeral at your church. If you do have the opportunity to usher at a funeral, a couple of special features will be added to your normal ushering responsibilities.

Most funerals, even those in your church, will be done under the guidance of a funeral director. You may need to help him locate items in the sanctuary such as lights, the controls to the sound system, and the reserve markers for the pews. Your extra help will be appreciated.

Give special care and attention to the needs of the immediate family of the deceased. You may need to direct the family members from their cars as they arrive at the church to the reserved area in the sanctuary. In some cases, you may need to aid members of the family into the pews. Remember that the family will be giving their total attention to each other and may need your strong direction for minor details.

Be aware that many who attend the funeral will be in your church for the first time. They will not be aware of the facilities in the building or the layout of the sanctuary. Offer your help and direction as appropriate. Try to anticipate some of their obvious needs.

You may be called on at the last minute to help remove flowers from the sanctuary and take them to a truck going to the grave site. Be ready to help when you are requested.

Special events and emphases and both happy and sad occasions will demand an extra effort on your part. Just remember, you are an usher for all seasons.

8
The Head Usher

Throughout the pages of this book reference has been made to the head usher. The next three pages are specifically set aside for you if you are the head usher at your church.

As the head usher, you must know the roles, functions, and total responsibilities of the usher group you lead. In addition, you must organize, train, plan, evaluate, and encourage each usher in the group.

Organize the Ushers.—You need to maintain an organization within the group that allows them to function properly. You may have one or one hundred members in the group. The larger the group, the more need for an organization plan. You may find it necessary to have an organization that includes a secretary, team captains, and other helpers.

Keep the organization simple enough to be understood by the group and complex enough to ensure that your assigned tasks are completed.

Train the Ushers.—You will find in the last few pages of this book suggestions for training the ushers. Every usher, new or experienced, needs training and updating. One way to provide training is to give each usher a copy of this book and encourage the usher to read and learn.

Another method is to set aside time each year for a weekend retreat. You can bring the group to the church or take them to a retreat setting for the training.

Plan with the Ushers.—You must plan with the ushers if you expect them to give their best efforts. Each usher wants to have a part in making plans for the group. Set aside times during the year when you hear the group share their ideas. Ask the group to suggest ways their ushering can be improved. Determine with the group's help whether the organization is functioning properly.

Plan together for special events and emphases in the church when the ushers are called on to help. Keep all ushers informed about the positive or negative feedback you receive.

Evaluate the Ushers.—You should have an understanding with the ushers as they are enlisted that you will be evaluating their work. Ask the group to help you in establishing the evaluation standards. Then you need to evaluate each usher by the standards. Consider such yardsticks as absences, tardiness, complaints from church members and church staff, handling emergencies, and so forth.

Ask the group to establish standards whereby your performance can be evaluated.

All evaluations can be shared with the Personnel Committee of the church.

Encourage the Ushers.—Every usher will appreciate

an encouraging word from you. New ushers want to know whether they are performing as they should be. Experienced ushers do not want to be taken for granted. Consider the following as ways of encouraging the group:

- work with the pastor to create an annual "Usher Appreciation Day"
- plan an "Usher Appreciation Banquet"
- establish an Ushers' Room (a place to keep their materials)
- establish guidelines for and award "The Usher of the Year"

You are a leader, the leader of the ushers at your church. Be an example of what you expect all the ushers to be.

Usher Training Helps

The material on these last few pages is designed to be used by a person who is training ushers. Four one-hour sessions are provided. Usher trainers could be the head usher, the pastor, or an experienced usher.

Session 1

Purpose: To identify the roles and functions of a church usher and describe how these are performed in a local church.

Preparation: 1. Arrange the room in small groups of four or five. Place a piece of newsprint and felt-tip markers in each group. 2. Write on a chalkboard, "Why did you accept the position of usher?"

Procedure:

1. As ushers arrive, send them into the small groups you have arranged. Direct the groups' attention to a statement on the chalkboard. After the ushers have shared with their small groups, ask for volunteers to share thoughts with the entire group.

2. Define the word *role* and relate it to the church usher. Assign the small groups to brainstorm and identify the roles of an usher. Suggest that the groups

record their findings on the newsprint. Call on a representative from each group to share the group's list. Tape each group's list to the wall.

When all groups have responded, create one master list by marking out similar responses. Indicate the four roles described in the book and compare these with the group-created list. Discuss any major differences.

3. Define the word *function* and relate it to the church usher. This time, ask the entire group to suggest ideas which describe the functions of an usher. Compare the findings with the material in the book and discuss any differences.

Read or tell the illustration of Usher Cook and the Harrises, asking the group to identify role and function examples. If the church has a role and function statement for the usher, consider sharing and discussing it with the group.

4. Share and discuss the section "Consider the Responsibilities."

5. Ask the group to respond to this question: What opportunities will you have because you are serving as an usher? Add to the sharing some thoughts for the section "Your Place to Serve."

6. Call on an usher to dismiss the group with a prayer of dedication.

Session 2

Purpose: To explore a wide range of qualities from which an usher can determine those he possesses and discover at least three he can develop.

Preparation: 1. Write the purpose statement on a

chalkboard. 2. Make three posters, lettering each one with one of the three groups of qualities mentioned in the book. 3. Invite your pastor to share in Step 5. 4. Have a supply of index cards ready for Step 6.

Procedure:

1. Using the illustration at the beginning of the chapter, introduce the purpose of this session. Call attention to the statement on the chalkboard. Underline the word *possess* and suggest that each usher already has many fine qualities. Circle the last phrase of the statement and indicate this as a challenge for each usher.

2. Make an introductory remark about each group of qualities. Attach the three posters to the wall at the appropriate times during your remarks.

3. Lecture briefly on each of the six qualities listed under "Qualities You Can't Do Without." Add your own comments and illustrations to those in the book as you teach. You may want to direct questions to the group at various points during your lecture.

4. Send the ushers into small groups with the following assignments: Study a quality ("Qualities You May Need to Develop") with your group and act it out before the large group. You may need to be selective in the assignments if your group is small. Or you may need to assign the same quality to a number of groups if your group is large.

5. Call on your pastor to represent the church membership in sharing "Qualities Others Expect You to Have." In addition to the content in the book, the pastor may want to add other thoughts and challenges.

6. Give an index card to each usher, asking each to write three qualities he is willing to work to develop during the year. Call on the pastor to close with a prayer of challenge for the ushers.

Session 3

Purpose: To examine and discuss the responsibilities of an usher before, during, and after the worship service and observe demonstrations of various responsibilities.

Preparation: 1. Plan to meet in the sanctuary for this session. 2. Write the assignments for Step 2 on the chalkboard. 3. Prepare a packet of material for each usher that includes a checklist form, floor plan forms, a church bulletin, an usher report form, and other forms used by the ushers.

Procedure:

1. Explain to the group that this session examines the total responsibility of the usher at a worship service: before, during, and after.

2. Send the ushers into three groups with the following assignments: *Group 1.*—Study and discuss the contents of chapter 3. Be prepared to share with the large group the highlights of the chapter and be prepared to properly demonstrate the responsibilities mentioned in the chapter. *Group 2.*—The same assignment as Group 1, but use chapter 4. *Group 3.*— The same assignment as Group 1, but use chapter 5.

Indicate that each group will have twenty minutes for study and twelve minutes to share and demonstrate.

3. Call the small groups into a large group. Ask

each group to share and demonstrate. If the reports do not cover all information in the chapters, challenge the ushers to study each chapter individually later for a full picture of their responsibilities. Call attention to the content in chapter 7, "Ushers for All Seasons."

If you have more than an hour available for this session, walk through the vestibule and sanctuary, pointing out the placement of various items such as light switches, control boxes for equipment, temperature controls, and storage areas for needed items.

4. Distribute the packet of forms and explain each form as time allows. Encourage the new ushers to study each form and ask for clarification later, if needed.

5. Close the session with a prayer of challenge for the ushers to be the best they can be as they serve their Lord and their church.

Session 4

Purpose: To hear and participate in a discussion of handling unexpected situations and to practice bringing emergencies under control.

Preparation: 1. Write the purpose statement on a chalkboard. 2. Create a placard for each of the five items listed under "Things to Do." 3. Type or write each of the seven emergencies on an individual card (see "Practice Handling Emergencies"). 4. Assign an experienced usher three minutes to share: Why it's important to talk with other ushers.

Procedure:

1. Ask the question: What is an emergency? After a

number of responses are given, call attention to the statement on the chalkboard.

2. Create a discussion atmosphere by asking a direct question related to the items on the placards. For example: How can you be prepared to act when an emergency occurs? Inject ideas and thoughts from the book as each item is discussed. Move through all five placards.

3. Move to the chalkboard and ask the group to brainstorm the question, What are some things you need to know to properly handle an emergency? When the ideas stop coming, ask the group to help you put the suggestions under three categories: What? Where? Who? Add to the lists ideas suggested in the book which have not been mentioned.

4. Divide the large group into a number of small groups (seven if possible). Give each group one of the emergencies described under "Practice Handling Emergencies." If you have prepared cards, hand a card to each group. Assign each group to (1) read the card, (2) respond to the emergency, and (3) share with the large group how an usher could respond to and bring the emergency under control.

Call on the small groups to share their findings.

5. Introduce the usher you have enlisted to share a three-minute talk.

6. Close the session with a prayer that each usher will always be prepared to handle emergencies.